$16.95

MW00559420

DIVIDUUM

SEMIOTEXT(E) FOREIGN AGENTS SERIES

© Gerald Raunig, 2016

Published by Semiotext(e)
PO BOX 629. South Pasadena, CA 91031
www.semiotexte.com

Copy Editing by Kelly Mulvaney and John Ebert.

Cover art by George Porcari. "Greetings From LA: Civic Center 2006." 2015. 46 x 32 inches.

Design by Hedi El Kholti

ISBN: 978-1-58435-180-1
Distributed by The MIT Press, Cambridge, Mass. and London, England
Printed in the United States of America

DIVIDUUM

MACHINIC CAPITALISM

AND MOLECULAR REVOLUTION

VOL. 1

Gerald Raunig

Translated by Aileen Derieg

\<e\>

CONTENTS

I. DIVIDUUM

Every Beginning is Dividual.

Just as the authorship of any book is divided, as all thinking always already stands on the shoulders of giants, who are obligated in turn to entire swarms of averagely tall people and allegedly negligible entities, as an intellect is inhabited by many ghosts, is never solely individual, everything begins in the raging middle of the dividual. The middle is raging, because in it things pick up speed, a stream overflowing in all directions, the opposite of regulated mainstream, mediocrity and mediation. The middle is not simply along the way between a beginning and an end; linearity and myths of origins are sucked into its maelstroms. The middle is dividual, because it implies parting the parts. Even if a "me" speaks here, this me has never been entirely alone. Divided and dividing, this instituent me shares its becoming with many instances of beginning in the middle.

The raging middle of the dividual applies not only to writing and speaking, the text-machines, the academic machines, the literary desiring machines. The body machines, the social machines, the revolutionary machines, the abstract machines, and their mutual con- and disjunctions also meet and separate in the dividual middle. Beginning in the middle, not at a point, but rather on the line. Drawing the line and being drawn by it, balancing on it in the midst of struggles. Four types of writing, and the beginning not only of writing is found in the middle. As in the case of Kalle Ypsilon.

After winning the election for state parliament, the candidate appears before the press, expresses her thanks and declares that social democracy is here again. Kalle Ypsilon stands behind her to the right in the row of supporters, as her life partner and closest advisor, sweating a bit and with his tie loosened, completely captivated by the moment. Machinically, he speaks the candidate's words along with her, initially with reserve, then with increasing vivacity, co-phrasing every emphasis, even anticipating the waves of applause. Word for word, in perfect accord, lip-syncing the candidate, he hurls the text toward the cheering audience. He stands so close to the candidate in the double brightness of spotlights and camera flashes that probably everyone notices—the press photographers, the journalists, everyone present, but also and especially the many television viewers following the first appearance of the election winner live. The only one who does not notice is Kalle Ypsilon, who continues speaking along with high concentration and enthusiasm—not bereft of his senses, but obsessed by many ghosts.

Authoritative writing is based on a paradox that is obscured especially because it is omnipresent. On the one hand it posits a beginning, a start that desires to be at the beginning. It is *a* beginning, and the subjective figure of this beginning is the author-individual. To be able to simulate a beginning as absolute, this individual has erased the multitude from which it comes, its molecular multiplicity, the many parts it shared before positing itself as undivided and indivisible. At the same time, and on the other hand, with finely tuned cross-references, quotations and proofs, the authorial individual establishes a lineage, a vertical connection to forefathers, back to an origin which appears far prior to all becoming that spreads out here and now. The filiation, the reference of the son to the father in a graduated sequence is nothing other than a molar parody of the erased multitude. The lineage is intended to strengthen the myth of the authorial individual, and it is paradoxically also proof that the authority seeks to be not only a beginning, but also always already there, a beginningless cause, "natural authority."

This "natural authority" as lineage and line of origin is seated next to and above the beginning of individual authorship as *auctoritas*. It claims authority implicitly or explicitly as a hierarchical positioning, molar reterritorialization, vertical linearity. A ladder that does not stand on the unstable floating ground of the middle, freely reaching up into the sky, but instead reaches from the ground of its origin straight to the wall. The authorial writer-individual stands on the last rung of the ladder facing the wall, pushing the ladder onto the ground with stiff feet, raising the ladder up to the wall with cramping toes. The ladder of lineage wants to be held against the ground of its origin and against the wall of what it has to show at the same time, to embody the origin and the *spectaculum* of the individual face.

Filiation, "natural authority," spirit of possession and anxious greed for letters domesticates text production, reduces the possibilities of content and form and compulsively striates modes of writing. As the corset of writing is pulled tighter and tighter, even the last wish for a different text is suffocated. Its place is taken by an insatiable desire for names and faces. They are the central function of authoritative writing, which arranges, subordinates, overcodes the text and its multiplicities. With face to the wall, name inscribes itself in the whiteness of this wall.

In the logic of authoritative writing, the failure of the Social Democratic candidate is not found in any political alliances that are false because they are too radical, but rather in that she does not manage to establish a distinguishable, individual authorship. She can no longer rid herself of the ghosts of the election machine she invoked. Where the author is no longer distinguishable, there is an even greater desire to produce an undivided author-subject, even if in reception. The question of the face behind the masks, of the identity behind the many layers, is a repetition of the desire for the father behind the son. Where production does not reveal names, reception works on the construction of a lineage. The initially inhibited, misplaced, in/visible co-author Kalle Ypsilon, shadow-man, human teleprompter, only seems to appear at the wrong moment and in the wrong place in the bright spotlights. From the perspective of authoritative writing, Kalle Ypsilon is the true author, the one who—unwittingly—reveals his authorship as ghost writer, the authority of the man behind the woman. And then it is all too easy for other uninvited ghosts, commentators in the mainstream media and, following them, the many posts in social media, to attack the candidate, to deride her as a female politician who cannot even come up with the simplest political platitudes by herself. This reading insinuates: "The woman can't even talk, but next to her is a man who tells her what to do." Ventriloquist doll, marionette, dummy, in their gender asymmetry all these images are a specially gendered variation of the principle of lineage, which has taken over molecular multiplicity. In the logic of authoritative writing there can only be one author, as significantly distinguishable as possible, and his name in this case is Kalle Ypsilon. Even if he is not the master in his house of ghosts, an individual, but by no means autonomous, Kalle's appearance is read under the auspices of authoritative writing. Where the undivided author-function does not come to light by itself, it is produced.

The second type is that of communitarian writing. As a mirror counterpart to individual-authoritative writing, it emphasizes common authorship. Counter to the liberal ideology of the individual and its moral evisceration of collectivity in the lineage, communitarian writing seeks to emphasize the General Intellect, common authorship, collective cooperation, from which not only knowledge and text production start. Here it is the community that is at the beginning, the communitarian-collective writing against individual-authoritative writing. Com-munitarian writing, however, must provide a *munus*, a tribute, make a sacrifice, in order to communally overcome the authoritative individual. Something is lost in sublating the author in the community. The individual author is threatened here by a very specific death, also a different death from the one foreseen by Foucault and Barthes forty, fifty years ago. Whereas poststructural interpretations affirm polyvocality, the multiplication of voices, proliferation of authorship, the author of communitarian writing is in danger of perishing in the whole, the unity, the uniformity of the collective. The *munus* of communitarian writing sinks the undivided-indivisible individual in the all-one.

Communitarian writing includes legal-type texts, political announcements, calls for solidarity, manifestos, but also more complex text formats that not only invoke the whole, the all-one, but also reproduce it in their form. Throwing out the baby with the bathwater here by abandoning the individual-one for the all-one also means losing the singular-one. Communitarian writing seeks to overcome individuality, and in so doing it runs the risk of weakening the manifold styles, the obstinacy, the specific nuances of theoretical and poetic architectures. The collective-communitarian type of writing gives rise to impreciseness, generalizations and standardizations. The community as beginning and as end devours not only the authoritative individual, it devours the singularities, too.

Authoritative and communitarian writing share their beginning at a uniform cause and their aim at a uniform goal. The one and universal substance determines the one author and the many units of communitarian writing. And in the end, the communitarian may perhaps be just as authoritative as the individual in a different way, by positing the community as the beginning, in the filiation of the community in reference to the construction of its prehistory, in the valorization of the name, now just a brand, a collective name. Just as natural and individual authority drives the many into the white wall, so does the communitarian with the singular.

Out of the mirroring problems of authoritative-individual and communitarian writing, the question of a different writing arises, which erases neither molecular multiplicity nor specific singularities. Is it possible to imagine contrasting the individual less with the communitarian, the collectivist, the community, and instead with the positive of the negative that is linguistically depicted with the concept of the in-dividual?

In search of dividual writing, my gaze falls first on its dark side, the third type, which I would like to call a type of interactive and activating writing. The becoming-machinic of capitalism implies a process of the increasing obligation and self-obligation of the parts to participate. This imperative of involvement, engagement and self-activation marks the entanglements and comprehensive valorizations in machinic capitalism, without clear boundaries between reception and production.

Already on what appears to be the purely receptive side of the text, there is an attempt to make exploitable the potentials of readers as consumers in the digital age of the book. In electronic reading machines, e-books and e-readers, technical platforms obtain extensive information about the readers' behaviors in relation to individual readings and modes of reading. This machinically readable data is significant for a continuum of exploitation, from the anonymous collection of big data to automatized-personalized advertising. Amazon meanwhile knows more about me than the state. I probably still buy the most interesting books in small, radical or obscure bookshops, but the mainstream books I look at online and sometimes order from Amazon should be sufficient to compile an ample profile. Were I able to use Kindle, even my personal notes could be stored electronically and would be visible for Amazon. This would yield, in typical market research jargon, my "reading behavior." Research into reading behavior is the invention of the glass reader—Amazon knows how much of a book someone like me reads, how fast someone like me reads it, which passages someone like me highlights, which passages someone like me euphorically comments on, where someone like me halts, and much more.

Data that is machinically readable and collectable can thus recursively affect the production of books, of texts altogether. It is possible, for example, to evaluate the collected data about passages frequently marked in e-books, or conversely about the points where reading is left off. The result on the production side is not simply that books that do not sell well are no longer published, but that authors are called upon to abridge books at points proven by data accumulation to be problematic or even re-write them. Individual attention comes into play once error on the part of the author has been democratically proven, when it ultimately becomes official that a significant portion of the readers give up reading a book I have written at a certain point. This information from Amazon's data holdings *operated by an automatic moderator* will be communicated for a fee by a start-up company to my publishing company, which will then approach me about it. Thanks to Amazon, in the future I may be requested to re-write just this one passage for the next English edition, abridge something here and there, maybe to prepare a short version altogether, which corresponds to about a quarter of the original text and is finally crowned by a spectacular title selected after surveying the readers—all of this, of course, on the objective data foundation of the "reading behavior" of "my" readers. And this, in principle, in an endless feedback loop and chain of ever new versions, which make the book appear to be an eternally unfinished work. From the slogan of the open art work it is only a small step to the Sisyphean nightmare of the now necessarily interactive author, who undergoes a new form of machinic subservience. Perpetually connected to the machine, the anonymous data-public governs over interactive writing.

The consumers can ultimately also be activated beyond these exploitation mechanisms and included in the middle of this processual co-writing. Experiments in this direction are already trying to probe the potential of co-writing readers on the Internet. Electronic voting about the futures of protagonists of books and screenplays are only the first test arrangements that potentially make the interactive in-between of the production stream accessible for exploitation as well. In the combinations of interactive reading permanently connected to the machine and crowd-activating writing, both individual positions and collected data are made utilizable. Valorized, subservient General Intellect, which like its counterpart, the wired and data-ized body, cannot find rest and must always keep moving through the endless expanses of inter-activity.

The goal could be imagined as an inversion of the old improv theater: it is no longer the few actors on stage that become active in response to spontaneous key words from the audience, but rather the function of the author-actors is limited to animating the many to conduct and utilize themselves in co-writing, participation, self-guidance. On the basis of this valorization of the swarm, the surplus of visibility occasionally falls in the end on the individual author again, who then also receives praise for having activated the swarm, the mob, the many, and also for taming them at the same time. Enveloping, enclosing activation that undermines every excess, normalizes it, or votes it out.

How will, in machinic capitalism, the middle become newly noncompliant? The text-machines are not simply means to political ends, propaganda tools, objects of revolutionary subjects. Text and revolution, critical discursivity and social struggles, text-machines and revolutionary machines cannot be understood as being external to one another. If a new social composition emerges in disobedience against machinic capitalism, new concepts are invented, and the texts are recomposed. Yet these concatenations undergo shifts in their different historical and geopolitical contexts. The occidental medieval concatenation of textual criticism and social machine, for instance, undoubtedly took place in a mode different from the counterpart of an economic power so difficult to grasp as that of industrial capitalism of the nineteenth century. The public intellectual of the late nineteenth and the twentieth century, from Zola to Sartre, was undoubtedly never entirely the heroic figure he imagined he was. Today, though, he is nothing more than a function of the media, an entirely subservient relic of the idea of the authoritative individual, which neatly fits into the respective media framework as soon as it is bid onto the public stage. Brave new world of philosophers in ever new poses of spectacular provocation and self-staging.

New challenges emerge when the position of the General Intellect, of a mass, multiple and militant intellectuality, is negotiated today. The intellect that does not close itself off in the single author-individual, the intellect that does not sublate the flows of social knowledge in a communitarian, general, universal unity, invents itself in machinic capitalism as a transversal intellect. This intellect is transversal, because it emerges in traversing the singularities of thinking, speaking, writing, fabricating knowledge: a machinic-dividual stream of thinking that moves across the dichotomy of individual and community, permeates individuals and collectives, inhabits the spaces, things, landscapes between them and allows new forms of disobedience to emerge, new forms of noncompliance, new dissemblages.

For the typology of writing, this means designating a fourth and final type, that of dividual writing. Its beginning lies in the middle, and regardless of how solitary a process it may appear to be, the writer is never entirely alone. There is the aforementioned effect of "standing on the shoulders of giants," the fact that genealogical lines are dis/connected in all writing. Genealogy is not at all to be equated with filiation, with the differenceless reference to the fathers, with the erasure of molecular multiplicity by the molar authority of lineage. Instead there is a hint here that the middle, into which every beginning sets itself, has never been an empty middle. No neutral vessel, but rather a middle, in which secret transactions happen, in which asymmetries spread out and dominant hierarchizations take place, as well as manifold empowerments. A diachronous and synchronous co-authorship of many in social space and in the a-linear depth of time has always been the basis of all writing. It is not only the real exchange among writers that plays a role, the mutual reading, commenting, discussing, the collegial critique, but also the exchange that is not or not yet completed, the wish production, the desire for the return and becoming of molecular multiplicity.

As in machinic capitalism knowledge production is valorized and writing is activated, we do not only have to deconstruct the myth of the genius, individual *auctoritas* as beginning, but primarily invent ways in which the now transversal intellect, writing as a dividual practice, as emancipatory, as not governed *in that way*, as not valorized *in that way*, can develop cooperations that are not compliant *in that way*.

"My condition," wrote Franz Kafka in the middle of a writing crisis in an early diary entry from 1910, "is not unhappiness, but it is also not happiness, not indifference, not weakness, not fatigue, not another interest—so what is it then? That I do not know this is probably connected with my inability to write. And without knowing the reason for it, I believe I understand the latter. All those things, that is to say, those things which occur to me, occur to me not from the root up but rather only from somewhere about their middle. Let someone then attempt to seize them, let someone attempt to seize a blade of grass and hold fast to it when it begins to grow only from the middle. There are some people who can do this, probably Japanese jugglers, for example, who scramble up a ladder that does not rest on the ground but on the raised soles of someone half lying on the ground, and which does not lean against a wall but just goes up into the air. I cannot do this—aside from the fact that my ladder does not even have those soles at its disposal."

As long as the dividual machine Kafka imagines itself individually isolated in the writing crisis, it will remain unable to write. The individual Kafka is standing on the last rung of his ladder, which is itself standing on the ground and against the wall. Ground of origin, white wall of representation and the face of the author-individual. It is only the creation of the dividual machine, in which the ladder and soles, the bodies of the jugglers, the many components of the machine resonate and become dissonant, which allows grass to grow from the middle of the blade. A dividual machine, divisible and dividing. There in the raging middle of the dividual, no ground is needed, no roots, no floor, no walls holding the ladder, no walls showing faces. The body-machines, the social machines, the revolutionary machines, the abstract machines separate there and meet with the text-machines; that is where the dividual-abstract line emerges from manifold ghostly hands.

Kafka's diary from 1910 again: "But every day at least one line should be trained on me, as they now train telescopes on comets. And if then I should appear before that sentence once, lured by that sentence ..."—the sentence comes from the dividual middle and is trained on and against the writer, who ends up in the cross-hairs, as a project, as projectile. It is multiplicity from which the sentence fires and is fired. The writer appears before the dividual sentence as though before a nameless court. The luring of this sentence is what lures the writer to write. Disbanding and bonding, stealing away and looking for a weapon, dis/connecting multiplicity and singularity. In the confusion of voices, in the crowd of ghosts, a line can be drawn, a weapon can be found. And thus ends Kafka's last diary entry from June 1923, about the difficulties of writing again, about the "hands of the ghosts," when every word twisted in their hands becomes a spear against the writer: "The only consolation would be: it happens whether you like or no. And what you like is of infinitesimally little help. More than consolation is: You too have weapons."

Why have I kept my name? Not just out of habit, pure habit, not only to make myself recognizable to the point of unrecognizability, not only to reach the point where it is no longer of any importance whether I say me or not. With all the problems of the molar aspects of an authoritative introduction and its representative logic: the me that speaks here wants to be a line that divides the multiplicity it comes from and affirms it at the same time. No erasure, but repetition of multiplicity. Pseudonyms, multiple names, bifurcations and fictionalizations of the me, condividualities, all of that can occur so long as the me does not make use of the fetish of the name. Leaving the posts, leaving no images behind, covering the tracks, betraying the name. But not in favor of anonymity, not into invisibility. Vanishing from the framework of organic representation, yes; erasing singularity, no.

"Machinically, he speaks the words of the candidate along with her." Machinic speaking-with, dividing-with, being-with, appending-with. Kalle Ypsilon is no author-individual, but a component of a dividual machine. And the Social Democratic candidate is no more just a marionette for which Kalle holds the strings than Kalle is a professional ghost-writer or a patriarchal ghost watching over the body of the candidate. A marionette theater that has lost the puppeteer pulling the strings, a machine with no machinist. Kalle and the candidate share not only everyday family life, a household and a professional-political working life, but also a house with many ghosts. Divided, divisible, dividing dividuality that affirms and concatenates the parts instead of isolating and unifying them. Head through the wall, ladder through the floor. No one rules the multitude of ghosts, no Holy Ghost controls the many voices, no father governs the sons.

[: Ritornello 1: et. al. Thanks :]

[: Together Isabell Lorey and I watched the candidate's appearance on television, were astonished by Kalle's speaking-with, laughed and were annoyed at the same time, could not believe it, discussed the media commentaries—and meanwhile, several years later, I verbalized to her my first steps of reinterpreting that media experience, discussed with her the problematic aspects of the whole thing, and I share with her the fantastic experience of taking off and flying, as well as possibly with some others too: Christoph Brunner, Ronald Burger, Aileen Derieg, Emma Dowling, Marcelo Expósito, Montserrat Galcerán, Anna Frei, Martina Fritschy, Pascal Gielen, Stefano Harney, Andrea Hummer, Bernhard Hummer, Alain Kessi, Niki Kubaczek, Brigitta Kuster, Sandra Lang, Nikolaus Linder, Artemy Magun, Birgit Mennel, Raimund Minichbauer, Boyan Manchev, Randy Martin, Rastko Močnik, Kelly Mulvaney, Jean-Luc Nancy, Antonio Negri, Roberto Nigro, Stefan Nowotny, Michaela Ott, Nikos Papastergiadis, Alice Pechriggl, Pantxo Francesco Salvini, Raúl Sánchez Cedillo, Eran Schaerf, Mariette Schlitz and Bert Theis, Bea Schlingelhoff, Klaus Schönberger, Ruth Sonderegger.

Et al.? Unpublished manuscripts, artistic escapades, misunderstood scraps of lectures, heated discussions, overheard terms, precise readings and re-readings, revisions, re-revisions, nights of drinking. There are whole choirs of dwarves involved, hordes made of all possible genders, all mutually plagiarizing, copying, rewriting, writing on and beginning to serve themselves and the machine in the raging middle of the dividual. :]

Dividuom face! Sexual Violence and Domination
through Partition

Beginning differently could imply beginning with the *Thesaurus linguae latinae*. Here, in the comprehensive treasury of Latin vocabulary, the adjective *dividuus* is listed under three meanings: "*1. i.q. divisus (de pluribus rebus inter se vel de singulis in partes divisis), saepe i.q. dimidiatus, anceps, duplex sim. [...] 2. i.q. divisibilis (tt.philos.) [...] 3. neutr. sing. pro subst.*"[1] In the period of the history of language covered by the thesaurus (early Latin, classical Latin antiquity and late antiquity), *dividuus* appears first of all in the meaning "divided," "separated," specifically in reference to the division, separation of multiple things from one another as well as of single things divided into parts in both their material and their immaterial aspects. Secondly, it is found in the meaning of "divisible," "separable," especially in philosophical texts, such as Cicero, Calcidius or Augustine. Thirdly and finally, it appears sporadically as a neutral singular instead of a substantive, but then usually heteronomously in relation to other words: as a substantive adjective in the neutral singular, *dividuum* is only found a few times, mainly (for instance, with Plautus, Terence, and later with Augustine and Cyprianus Gallus) in the phrase *dividuum facere* instead of *dividere*.

Even though the word *dividuum* mainly appears in Latin as adjunct adjective, this third, heteronomous substantive case can be found at the beginning of the history of the word. The first appearances of *dividuum* occur in the neighboring zones of slavery and sexual violence, but also in a streaking trace of fugacity that flees these intersecting conditions of violence, allowing it to steal (into) freedom. The multiply graduated mixing ratios of extreme sexualized oppression, economic dependency and (in the best case) self-empowerment in/from sex work are where the lexical history of *dividuum* begins.

The first two documented occurrences are found in the comedies of Plautus and of Terence, the Latin *palliatae* performed in Greek garb toward the end of the third and in the second century before common era.[2] The *fabulae* or *comoediae palliatae* took their name from the *pallium*, the cloak-like garment worn by Greek actors (in contrast to the Roman *togata*). They transformed the material of the New Attic Comedy into Latin and into the Republican Roman context. Already a highly moral institution, this theater was also an institution for exercising economically framed relations of violence. Both areas, moral education and oikonomia, prove to be intertwined in the comedy material, especially in diverse transactions that often went far beyond the household, the *oikos*, the *domus* in the narrower sense. Whereas the political realm hardly played a role, morality and economy conjoined to make the center of the plots.

The oikonomic bias of the Roman comedy is often evident in details, also and especially in the first passages where the word *dividuum* appears. Money and goods are what is to be divided. Contracts and promises, breaches of contract and betrayals, interpretations of property rights and entanglements between different micro-markets and economic regimes unfold in the negotiations. Haggling over human goods invokes the logic of partition, and an appropriate vocabulary is needed for it as well. The *comoedia palliata*, in all its humor, travesty and accumulation of intrigues, primarily produces a moral discourse on the best partition, attribution, distribution.

Exercising the order of heteronormativity specific to antiquity, the plot of the comedies by Plautus and Terence is usually arranged around a heterosexual love story. The female part is often a slave in the hands of a *leno* (slave trader/pimp) and the object of various disputes. Young men free female slaves out of love or for a best friend, sometimes with the help of slaves belonging to the *domus* of the father, or they attempt to pay nothing or as little as possible for the slave's freedom. Intrigues, disguises and more or less successful frauds are strung together in multiple rounds. A recurring climax of the comedic plot is the *anagnorisis*, the "recognition" of the purported slave as the daughter of a free, respected citizen. This identification ritual liberates the woman from the "a-moral" power of the *leno*, while also placing her in another sphere of domination, that of the father and/or the potential husband. *Patria potestas* is exercised as power of control over the bodies, assets and economic productivity of the family. In multiple graduations it spreads out over the male and female members of the *domus*, but it is also in effect beyond its boundaries, as male slaves can also assume significant roles outside the *domus*.

In the finale of the comedy *Rudens* ("The Mooring Rope," first performed in 211 bce), Plautus has the older free citizen Daemones and the *leno* Labrax negotiate the release of a female slave. Although the moral of the comedy never leaves even a doubt that the slave should be released (whether because a free citizen has started a love relationship with her or because it turns out that she is the lost daughter of a citizen), the fundamental economic power relationship of slavery as a component of ancient Roman patriarchal rule is never called into question.[3]

Even though he seems to belong to a completely different world, the world of godlessness and infamy, the *leno* is part of these relations of power and violence. Whereas the word *leno* has been and is also trivializingly rendered as "panderer," his professional fields of occupation comprise activities between trafficking women and managing sex work.[4] The extent to which one spills over into the other can only be guessed at from the allusions in the ancient Roman comedies. It may be presumed, however, that despite all contextual differences there are similarities to the contemporary situation, that this gray zone was tolerated, indeed even socially produced. In *Rudens*, the *leno*, wholly in keeping with the attribution of his role, is depicted as a reprehensible figure corrupting youth, and Labrax is an especially stereotypical leno, deceitful, godless, perjurious.[5] Beyond this stereotype, though, his function is primarily that of an enterprising slaveholder and trader, seeking to advance his own interests regardless of any morality: both with respect to the slaves that he regards as property endangered from all sides and with respect to the free citizens and their slaves, who riddle his purely economic interest with their moral arguments in every particular case. This situation between property issues and (a)morality corresponds to the ambiguous social position of the *leno*: on the one hand, his status is that of *infamia*, he is constantly in danger of being ridiculed, cursed, beaten, even by slaves. On the other hand, he is allowed to go about his business without legal consequences.[6]

Rudens starts with the confusion after Labrax and two young women in his possession (*meae mulieres*), Palaestra and Ampelisca, have been shipwrecked. Following the wreck of the slave ship, the two women are able to flee in a boat to Cyrene and find the initial protection of a shrine to Venus and its priestess. In one of Labrax's trunks that was lost in the shipwreck there are clues that Palaestra is the daughter of the respected citizen Daemones, to whose properties the castaways come by various ways. In addition, the trunk holds all the money possessed by the *leno*. The twofold content of the trunk becomes the key to the release of both women. Palaestra is recognized by Daemones when she names the toys from her childhood in a scene of inquisition about the contents of the trunk, and Daemones recognizes her as his own daughter. The first solution thus consists of the class-specific version of liberation: the necessary condition for slavery is not given, because Palaestra's status following the recognition by her father is that of a free citizen. For Ampelisca, release must be effected differently.

Daemones' slave Gripus pulls the trunk out of the sea in his fishing net. He then demands the promised reward for finding it, but as a slave he can possess no property—he is not a legal subject and therefore requires prudent support from his *dominus*, Daemones, and his partitioning domination.[7] Strictly speaking, what the slave finds belongs to his lord. In the final scene of *Rudens*, Daemones grants Gripus his help, but not entirely in the way the slave had hoped for, such as allowing him to dispose of the reward at will. It is the *dominus* who undertakes the partitioning, giving the slave Gripus his part in negotiation with the *leno* Labrax and paying for Ampelisca's release with the reward at the same time:

Daemones: *Dic mihi, quanti illam emisti tuam alteram mulierculam, / Ampeliscam?*
Labrax: *Mille nummum denumeravi.*
D. *Vin tibi / condicionem luculentam ferre me?*
L. *Sane volo. /*
D. *Dividuom talentum faciam.*
L. *Bene facis.*
D. *Pro illa altera, / libera ut sit, dimidium tibi sume, dimidium huc cedo.* (Plaut. Rud. 1405–1409)"
D. Tell me, at what price did you buy that other young woman, Ampelisca?—
L. I paid down a thousand didrachms.—

D. Should you like me to make you a handsome offer?—

L. I should like it much.—

D. I'll divide the talent [*dividuom faciam*].—

L. You act fairly.—D. For that other woman Ampelisca, that she may be free, take one half, and give the other half to him."

What is at stake, on the whole, is the sum of a talent that the *leno* promised to pay for finding his trunk. Daemones determines the partition. His proposal is that half of the sum should be used to free Ampelisca, the other half given to Gripus as a finder's reward, so that he can also buy his freedom. "*Dividuom facere* (*dividuom* is the old Latin form of *dividuum*) the talent" means to make it divisible, to test the possibility of dividing it into two parts. More precisely, Daemones says *dividuom talentum faciam*. The grammatical subject reveals the power relations. The free citizen and *dominus* Daemones provides a solution to the problem to which everyone involved must agree. With his proposal he disposes of the reward as though he were both finder and owner at the same time. It does not count that Labrax is the owner of the trunk and that Gripus found it. All that counts is the authority of the partitioning lord.

Daemones' solution is partition. All parties are given their part, but it takes the moral-economic position of the *pater familias* to assume power extending beyond the *domus* and to determine and distribute the parts. This is a distribution of parts intended to demonstrate the *patria potestas* and the expanding rule of the patriarch as good and beneficent governing. The patriarch is the one who can remind the slave of his legal-economic impotence, the *leno* (paradoxically) of his moral obligation to pay the announced finder's reward. One side of the partition is that, with the purchase of Ampelisca's freedom, the first half flows into the treasury of the slave trader. The second half consists of buying the freedom of the slave Gripus, who is doubly dependent: he cannot simply demand and obtain his finder's reward; for this he needs the protective hand of the *pater familias*. From him he must also buy his freedom. Thus, the second half for the purchase of the slave's freedom ultimately benefits the patriarch's wealth.

Dividuom faciam is an extrajudicial judgment on the partition and distribution of the parts, which induces the happy end through the authority of the *pater familias* who pronounces it. No *deus ex machina* is needed: in the end the good patriarch resolves all entanglements in harmony, those of the enslaved women, the boys, the slaves, and even the realm of infamy. Multiply graduated asymmetry, partitive striation of the economic, renewed distribution of the social space, accumulation through partition.

Half a century later, in the last comedy by Terence, *Adelphoe* ("The Brothers," first performed in 160 bce), the word *dividuum* appears for the second time and again in a similar context of morality and economy. In the play about the contrary pedagogical relationships of two very different brothers (the permissive Micio and the authoritarian Demea) to their two sons, the tendencies described for Plautus' *Rudens* are even more clearly evident. Here too, everything revolves around the authority of partition against the backdrop of patriarchal rule.

Right at the beginning, the son raised permissively by Micio is introduced as a figure of *licentia*, ambiguous as a free spirit and feeling himself not bound by any laws. He appears as somebody who broke open the door of a stranger's house in broad daylight, kidnapped a woman and beat up the householder: the broken door and the beating are in the foreground of Demea's paternalistic discourse of protection. In the course of the story, however, it turns out that the householder is the *leno* Sannio, and the one son has robbed/rescued the other son's beloved from the violent context of sex work and slavery under the *leno*. The word *eripere* used in this passage (Ter. Ad. 90) appropriately means both "rob" and—especially in conjunction with slavery—"rescue" at the same time. The argument about the interpretation not so much of the word as of the action leads to a scene with structural similarities to the previously described passage from Plautus. Again there is a pimp/slave trader, Sannio, proverbially a "fool,"[8] again it is about freeing a female slave, and for the second time in the written records of the Latin language, the term *dividuom* appears. This time, however, the passage is relatively close to the beginning of the comedy, at the end of the second act, and thus still far from any happy end. Accordingly, the negotiations at this point are more complicated, as they are being conducted by actors who still do not have the status needed to resolve all complications and reaffirm the hierarchy in the economy of partition: Micio's slave Syrus is speaking to the *leno* Sannio.

> Syrus: *Unum hoc habeo: vide si satis placet: / Potius quam venias in periclum, Sannio, / servesne an perdas totum, dividuom face. /* (Ter. Ad. 239–241) "Syrus: I have this one proposal to make; see if you fully approve of it. Rather than you should run the risk, Sannio, of getting or losing the whole, halve it."

Dividuom face: The proposal appears here in a very early phase of the entanglements, and the grammatical subject and predicate are placed very differently from Plautus' finale. The "goods" have already been "stolen," it is a matter of preliminary negotiations to legitimize this action and fix the subsequent price. Here it is the bargaining slave who calls upon the slave trader to make a division. And Syrus points out to the *leno* that he risks losing everything (in the case of the female slave) and should therefore be satisfied with the half (of the sale price). Divide the whole! Halve it!

The halving division of the purchase amount meets with hard resistance. Foremost, however, *dividuom face* in this passage is lacking the essential authority of the partition economy. Whereas the glass appears to be half full to the *leno* Labrax in the final scene of Plautus' *Rudens*, here it looks half empty to the *leno* Sannio. Because his slave has been kidnapped, Sannio sees himself thwarted in his plan to organize the shipment of several recently purchased female slaves, in order to sell them far away from Athens for a profit. In the end, however, it all fits well as it fits to the rule of partition. In the shadow of the seemingly insurmountable opposition between permissive and authoritarian upbringing, the morality of the patriarchal partition remains unquestioned. Also in the case of the permissive father Micio, who explicitly emphasizes the difference between the respectful, fatherly *imperium* and the violent domination over slaves (Ter. Ad. 64–77), moral authority and money first enable partition. The good householder is the one who provides advice and help for his household and his subordinates, and where his authority does not apply, he boosts it with economic means.

In the moral performances of the Roman comedy, written from the perspective of the free citizen like all other available sources on slavery in antiquity, passive roles are attributed to the female figures, in between desperation and a need for help, dependent on the inscrutable plan of the gods and especially on *consilium* and *auxilium*, counsel and aid from free men. Whereas these discourses embrace the advantages of permissive upbringing, acts of liberation, a whole morality of freedom, the female figures remain quiet objects of partition. For female slaves, the only alternatives to their unfree life under the rule of the *leno* appear as two possible perspectives of heteronomous reterritorialization: integration and subordination in/to the oikonomic regime of the *pater familias* (with recognition as the clearest indication of this form of identificatory allocation and (re-)attribution of the part)—or being shipped off as a slave and relocated heteronomously in a remote place.

The comedies suggest that the economy of slavery and shipping already permeated the European-African geography of the Mediterranean in antiquity. In *Adelphoe* Sannio hastily plans to set off with his female slaves to bring them from Athens to Cyprus. In *Rudens* shipping is already well under way, as Labrax intends to bring the female slaves from Cyrene (a Greek colony in present-day Libya) to Sicily and is only prevented from doing so by shipwreck. From this perspective, the image of an uncharted space of violence emerges, entirely outside the realm of the grand narrative of the Punic Wars, which historiographically formed by far the most powerful foreign-policy narrative of the time when both comedies were written. The European-African Mediterranean of Greek-Roman antiquity, from the Roman perspective *mare nostrum*, "our sea," was not only the logistical space of the transfer of goods and war materiel. It may be conjectured that here, long before the invention of modern logistics in the shipping trade of the Atlantic slave trade, shipping was invented as a violent deterritorialization of slaves, necessarily followed by an equally violent reterritorialization in a new territory.

Alongside and below the impossible choice between two violent forms of heteronomous reterritorialization, alongside the stereotype attribution of gendered passivity in the comedies, even counter to the calculations of plots and authors, before their plans and behind their backs—the fleeing-streaking force of those who were actually supposed to remain quiet takes effect. This line of flight appears in *Rudens* when the two women take their fate into their own hands in the shipwreck and actualize the possibility of liberation from the life-threatening sea together. *Neque gubernator umquam potuit rectius*: "Not a helmsman could have ever done it better" (Plaut. Rud. 166), it is said about the landing maneuver of the two women.

From the situation of rupture, which goes beyond the shipwreck, together they draw a fragile line. This line of flight is by no means a straight line; it is winding and broken, and it has several stages, from the ship into the boat, from the boat to land, into the exile of the temple of Venus, and finally into the *domus* of Daemones.

The flight is inventive, but it is never a *creatio ex nihilo*. It does not invent anything from nothing, but instead resets and seeks to newly arrange the existing circumstances.[9] The order, arrangement, constitution of patriarchal partition that the women come upon is never called into question in its entirety in the narratives of Roman comedy. The specific story of reterritorialization is even in danger of reinforcing the constituted space of patriarchal partition, simply adding further striations to it, striating, individualizing, domesticating the common, streaking practice of the two women in the difference of recognition and the purchase of freedom. And yet the temporary deterritorialization of small flights indicates the possibility of a leap that goes beyond individual liberation and the reestablishment of paternal order. The last refuge is not the teleological goal in a chain of partial flights heading for release. Even though the narrative of the comedies does not allow for anything else in linear reception— becoming a free subject is not necessarily the women's final goal. The multiple instances of stealing away indicate the immanent search for other ways of living, other economic circumstances, other forms of cooperation.

The twofold meaning of *eripere* as "rob" and "rescue," as it occurs in *Adelphoe*, is a first indication of an understanding of stealing that more fundamentally undermines ownership relations, entirely counter to the logic of purchasing freedom and self-appropriation at an individual level. Stealing the brother's bride from the clutches of the *leno* still remains in the double logic/logistics between shipping off on the one hand and victimization and patriarchal partition on the other. The way Palaestra and Ampelisca steal away is different and more active, especially in fleeing across the water, before the two women find shelter in the asylum of the Venus Shrine.[10]

Beyond the logistics of heteronomous reterritorialization, the women's stealing (themselves) away in the shipwreck emerges as an incompliant subversion of property relations. The one who is shipped is always also a potential fugitive, even a potential smuggler, who, as Fred Moten says, is "carrying something—and what [s]he carries is, first and foremost, a kind of radical, non-locatability."[11] The knowledge of freedom emerges in the invention of flight, in the act of drawing the line of flight out of slavery, but also out of the oikonomic-moral rule of partition. Stealing away, reinterpreting the shipwreck as a break with slavery, which simultaneously gains, coerces, steals freedom, but not in the sense of appropriation, of self-possession, of an individual possessing itself and its territory.

[: Ritornello 2: Queering Space, Time, Domination :]

[: Crossing right through space, through time, through becoming and past. Eternal queer return. An eighty-thousand or roughly 368-year-old being traversing multiple individuals, multiple genders, one after another and at the same time, through asymmetries in time and space and beyond, even in the most extreme fate, in spaces of violence and relations of domination. In the sea and ashore, *while one drowns us the other gnaws us*, flood and beast. *If we survive the waves, we succumb to the teeth.* And yet, right there, where it becomes hopeless and unambiguous, where there *can be no doubt of the sex*, is a stealing away, along an etymological line of "transverse," from the German word "quer" and the English "queer" back to the Middle High German word *twër*, derived in turn from the verb *twërn* for turning, reversing, stirring, mixing. This verb seems to be related to the Latin *vertere*, which has a very similar set of meanings: turn, revolve, reverse. And who knows what wonderful oddities the secret scholars of the Indo-European might be able to invent before, between and beyond any recognizable relationship. Within the spell of this conceptual field we also find the word, often used colloquially in Romance languages, transversal. Queer wish production, trans-reason, trans/versal intellect, not the portrait of Dorian Gray, but rather the overflowing, fragmentary biography of Orlando, interrupted by weeks of sleep, deviating from the straight line of life. With its singular *measure of value*, the *transreason of passion* also and especially reaches the darkest, most remote margins. It focuses on *exceptions, on things that leave most people cold and seem to lack sweetness.* Exception, singularity, gaiety. *And indeed, it cannot be denied that the most successful practitioners of the art of life, often unknown people by the way, somehow contrive to synchronize the sixty or seventy different times which beat simultaneously in every human organism. Of the rest, some we know to be dead, though they walk among us; some are not yet born, though they go through the forms of life; others are hundreds of years old though they call themselves thirty-six.* Multiplicity of me's, synchronous and diachronous, turning cartwheels through the millennia and through endless worlds. Instead of an intellect imprisoned in spirit, rather a *transreason of passion haunted by ghosts,* crossing through the transversal intellect throughout genders, voices, landscapes—freaks, burlesques, Damenkraft. :]

The Philosophy of In-/Divisibility

Beginning differently could begin with the world, or the question of whether the world has a beginning or not, and if not, whether the world, if it has no beginning, does have a becoming. This is one of the questions of Plato's *Timaeus*, which Cicero translated into Latin in 45 bce. In Cicero's philosophical works of that year, the term *individuum* occurs in various contexts and meanings. In keeping with the habits of the conventional understanding of language, *individuum* would be understood as a Latin word, where the prefix *in-* indicates the negation of the word *dividuum* formed prior to it. Yet already in Latin philosophy, *individuum* is placed equiprimordially alongside *dividuum* as a quasi absolute word, resulting in the suppression of its positive. There are three philosophical strands that suggest *individuum* as a translation from Greek into Latin. These are, first of all, the Democritic strand of the atomic theory with its translation of *atomos* as *individuum*, as undivided particle; then there is the Platonic strand with *individuum* as the indivisibility of being; and finally, beginning in late antiquity, there is the Aristotelian strand developing *individuum* as a logical figure, which in conjunction with the Platonic strand is influential in the doctrine of the trinity and christology.

In Cicero's philosophical writing from the year 45 BCE, first the Democritic strand is evident. Democritus' atomic theory conceptualizes the world as a mass of endless matter from countless, dissimilar, immutable and indivisible particles. The movement of the atoms can only be understood in contrast to a boundless space, the "void." Through their uniformity, atoms mutually affect one another by colliding, and in their assemblages they form all things, which are distinguished through the shape, arrangement and situation of the assembled atoms. Cicero's theory is marked by a lifelong rejection of the Democritic theories, especially Epicureanism. Only Plutarch's attacks on Epicurus, written around 100 bce, surpass the impact of Cicero's negative reading of Epicurean thinking. It is possible that both used the same source hostile to Epicurus in their polemics.

In his writings on Greek philosophy, Cicero repeatedly refers polemically to Epicurus and his central positions of radical immanence, the enhancement of pleasure in life, the surmountability of fear and superstition. Cicero starts the five books *De finibus bonorum et malorum* with a fundamental defense of the translation of Greek philosophy into Latin. The subsequent extended treatise on Epicurean ethics is prefaced by a brief sweeping criticism of Epicurus' philosophy (Cic. fin. 1,17–26). At the beginning of this passage Cicero introduces the term *individuum* as the translation of the word *atomos* from Greek. He begins his explanation of the Epicurean theory with the translation of Democritus' definition of the atom:

> *ille atomos quas appellat, id est corpora individua propter soliditatem, censet in infinito inani, in quo nihil nec summum nec infimum nec medium nec ultimum nec extremum sit, ita ferri, ut concursionibus inter se cohaerescant, ex quo efficiantur ea, quae sint quaeque cernantur, omnia, eumque motum atomorum nullo a principio, sed ex aeterno tempore intellegi convenire* (Cic. fin. 1,17). "He [Democritus] says that what he calls atoms are, due to their density, indivisible bodies, in the endless void, in which there is nothing, no up, no down, no middle, no last, and no outside, which so move that they cohere with one another through collisions, so that out of this everything emerges that is and that

is perceived, and that it is right to understand the movement of the atoms as movement without beginning, since eternal time."

From this brief summary of Democritus' atomic theory it is evident that Cicero used the literal translation *atomus*, while also proposing to render the atoms in Latin as *corpora individua*, "indivisible bodies." With Lucretius and his comprehensive adaptation of the Democritic/ Epicurean atomism in the first Latin didactic poem, the atoms are still called *corpora prima* or *primordia* or *parvissima*. Whereas Lucretius thus highlights the primordiality of the smallest bodies, Cicero primarily emphasizes, alongside the density and opposition to the void, the indivisibility of the atoms.

The Cicero passage quoted above (fin. 1, 17) marks the first instance of the word *individuus*, which initially appears as an adjective. It returns again shortly thereafter, in conjunction with the discussion of Epicurean theory, in Cic. fin. 1, 18, and then substantively in 2, 75, as well as in Cicero's second extensive philo- sophical work, the *Tusculanae disputationes*. There, in a more general section on the Platonic theory of souls, Cicero investigates the after- life of the soul after death. Other philosophical theories about the soul and its im/mortality are also presented in a longer insertion, or—as in the case of the Democritic deviation—specifically not presented at all:

> *illam vero funditus eiciamus individuorum corporum levium et rutundorum concursionem fortuitam, quam tamen Democritus con- calefactam et spirabilem, id est animalem, esse volt* (Cic. Tusc. 1,42). "I do not want to discuss that planless collision of indivisible light and round bodies that Democritus nevertheless understands as being thoroughly warmed and animated, i.e. enlivened."

A few lines earlier Cicero had already commented disparagingly on this *concursio fortuita*, the planlessness, randomness of the collision of the atoms:

> *Democritum enim, magnum illum quidem virum, sed levibus et rotundis corpusculis efficientem animum concursu quodam fortuito, omittamus; nihil est enim apud istos, quod non atomorum turba conficiat* (Cic. Tusc. 1,22). "I will omit Democritus, undoubtedly a great man, according to whom, however, the soul is engendered from a planless collision of light and round particles; for his followers, there is nothing that a swarm of atoms could not effect."

The *turba*, the restless swarm of indivisible particles, the bustle and throng of the multitude, the eternal struggles and capabilities of the atoms are much too uncertain ideas for Cicero's stance on the becoming and passing of the soul.[12] Tumultuousness and the random meeting of endlessly many, eternally moving particles populating the void, the Democritic interplay of division, multitude and movement: none of this can be classified in Cicero's classical idea of a systematic design and animation through a force external to the atoms.

[: Ritornello 3: *The Desire of the Many,* or the Missing
Appendix to Karl Marx's Dissertation :]

*[: About pleasure it has been roughly said (that is, by Epicurus): their
theory … does in a way remove fear and superstition, but it gives no joy
or divine favor. The idea of such omnipotent agents, by contrast, was
always associated with the idea of fright. For whom the world appears
without reason, hence who is without reason himself, for him is god. Or
lack of reason is the existence of god. Plutarch does not understand the
fear of god at all in the sense that Epicurus does; he does not grasp how
philosophical consciousness wishes to free itself from it. Although the
Epicurean dialectic is wrongly criticized by Plutarch, his polemic can in
effect be called a panegyric in favor of Epicurus: in his polemic against
Epicurus, Plutarch teaches the Epicurean doctrine.*

*For them [the Epicureans] fleeing from evil is happiness and goodness.
The essence of what is good arises from the flight from evil, from its
memory, reflection and the joy that one has encountered it. For what produces untamable joy is the feeling that one has escaped a great evil. Yet
Plutarch fails to understand the logic of Epicurus. Indeed, Epicurus desires
no eternal life: how much less can it matter to him that the next instant
may conceal some misfortune. Fear of the future, that state of insecurity, is inserted into the remote consciousness of god, considered as a
condition which pre-exists in him, but also in the first place as a threat.*

*The lowest class makes no pretensions, the second weeps and wants to do
anything to save atomistic being, the third is the philistine who
exclaims, my god, but that would be even better!* adikoi kai poneroi,
"the unjust and wicked ones," epikeinoi kai noun echontoi, *"the*

decent and reasonable ones," and in between hoi polloi kai idiotoi, *"the many and single ones."*

For the *"unjust and wicked," fear is adduced as a means of improvement. Yet it is the hell of the populace. Plutarch thinks himself very wise when he says that besides necessity, which means fleeing from evil, the animal seeks the good that lies beyond the flight. Its animal nature lies precisely in the seeking of a good in the beyond. According to Epicurus, no good for man lies outside himself. Criminals and transgressors of the law, they say, pass their entire lives in misery and apprehension, since even though they may succeed in escaping detection, they can have no assurance of doing so; in consequence fear for the future lies heavy on them and precludes any delight or confidence in their present situation.*

The arrogance of the elected is that of the class of the "decent and reasonable": needless to say, it by no means surpasses the preceding. Rather, what at first appeared as animal fear now appears in the form of arrogance, of demand, of entitlement. So these good and clever men expect the reward of life after life. What a demand! The bad must recognize them in life as the good ones, and they themselves do not even recognize as good the universal powers of life! Is that not the pride of the atom screwed onto the highest pitch? Hence this class, as Plutarch describes it, departs most of all from reason.

We now arrive at the view of the polloi, although it becomes apparent in the end that few do not share it, indeed, to be frank, all swear allegiance to this banner, reluctant to give up atomistic being. "The multitude, free from fear of what happens in Hades, have a myth-inspired expectation of eternal life; and the desire for being, the oldest and most powerful of all our passions, provides pleasure and bliss overcoming that childish terror." Plutarch is of the opinion that the name of change sounds more pleasant than that of completely ceasing to exist.

But the change must not be a qualitative one; the individual ego in its individual being must persist; the name is therefore only the sensuous presentation of that which it is, and is meant to signify the opposite. The thing must not be changed, but only put in a dark place, the interposition of fantastic remoteness is only intended to conceal the qualitative leap — and every qualitative difference is a leap.

We remind Herr Schelling of the last words of his letter: "The time has come to proclaim to the better part of humanity the freedom of minds, and not to tolerate any longer that they deplore the loss of their fetters." When the time already had come in 1795, how about the year 1841? Philosophy extends itself to the world, weaving, as though a practical person, intrigues with the world. The sustained, real crystallizations, the silent, persevering mole of real philosophical knowledge—that is the carnival of philosophy, whether it disguises itself as a dog like the Cynic, in priestly vestments like the Alexandrian or in fragrant spring array like the Epicurean. :]

The partly misunderstandable and misunderstanding, yet thoroughly skeptical presentation of Epicurus' natural philosophy and its Democritic background is the context, in which a first necessity for the placement of the word *individuum* arises for Cicero. The Platonic strand of the Latin term also starts with Cicero, in the translation of Plato's late writing *Timaeus* (around 360 bce), and this is also where the first philosophical appearance of the term *dividuum* occurs. Cicero probably did not plan to publish his *Timaeus* translation, but prepared it as an exercise for his own philosophical writings in the same year as *De finibus* and *Tusculanae disputationes* (45 bce). He translated about a quarter of the entire *Timaeus* text, primarily the central parts at the beginning of

Timaeus' speech. In these sections, in the course of several attempts, Plato's Timaeus discusses the creation of the world by the "creator god," the demiurge. His first approach applies to the creation of the world-body, the universe as an intelligent being, the second to the creation of the world-soul, intervals and time, and then—and still included in Cicero's translation—Timaeus comments on the ("younger," compared to the demiurge) Olympian gods and the migration of souls.

It takes Plato several attempts to describe a process that cannot be described in a linear manner. World-body and world-soul were not created one after another, and yet the form of philosophical treatise forces him into this sequence. In the first approach, he describes the creation of the world body, only to start again with the creation of the world-soul, which still is called the mistress and ruler of the body. This minor ambiguity in the hierarchy, which Timaeus also notes in his speech (Plat. Tim. 34b/c), indicates a greater theoretical problem, which necessarily accompanies the rigorous distinction between a beginningless, divine being and a subordinated, worldly becoming, which always implies beginning and cause. The idea that the cosmos is caused, evolved and yet nevertheless eternal is a problem that continued to influence the Christian theory of creation and the trinity.

In Cicero's translation the difference *dividuum–individuum* now appears in the central passage, where the demiurge creates the world-soul:

> *Ex ea materia, quae individua est et quae semper unius modi suique similis, et ex ea, quae in corporibus dividua gignitur, tertium materiae genus ex duobus in medium admiscuit, quod esset eiusdem naturae et quod alterius; idque interiecit inter individuum atque id, quod dividuum esset in corpore* (Cic. Tim. 21). "Out of the matter

that is indivisible [*individua*], always of a kind and self-similar, and out of the matter that emerges divisible [*dividua*] on the bodies, he mixed a third genus of matter formed out of the two in the middle, which should be of the same nature and of the other, and this he placed between the indivisible [*individuum*], and the divisible [*dividuum*] on the body."

This is the point in the history of philosophy, where the distinction between *individuum* and *dividuum* becomes explicit as a translation of indivisible and divisible matter. Cicero translates the difficult *Timaeus* passage rather superficially—in lieu of the difference between indivisible being and becoming divisibility, he simply inserts matter in both cases. In the original Greek, the same passage reads:

τῆς ἀμερίστου καὶ ἀεὶ κατὰ ταὐτὰ ἐχούσης οὐσίας καὶ τῆς αὖ περὶ τὰ σώματα γιγνομένης μεριστῆς τρίτον ἐξ ἀμφοῖν ἐν μέσῳ συνεκεράσατο οὐσίας εἶδος, τῆς τε ταὐτοῦ φύσεως αὖ πέρι καὶ τῆς τοῦ ἑτέρου, καὶ κατὰ ταὐτὰ συνέστησεν ἐν μέσῳ τοῦ τε ἀμεροῦς αὐτῶν καὶ τοῦ κατὰ τὰ σώματα μεριστοῦ (Plat. Tim. 35a). "Out of the indivisible and self-identical being, and out of the divisible being becoming in the bodies, he fused a third kind of being in the middle, partaking of the nature of the same and of the other, and placed it accordingly in the middle between the indivisible amongst them and the bodily divisible."

What is translated here as division is not the Greek *atomos*, as in the Democritic strand. Cicero translates *merístos* (from *méros*, part) as *dividuum*, and parallel to this *individuum* for *amerístos*. He passes over the difference between the unchangeable *ousía*/being (in the case of the indivisible) and the becoming of divisibility, using the reduced term of matter for both modes of being. According to

Timaeus' explanation, in order to conjoin the two modes of being, a third mode is needed, which consists primarily in the correct compound proportions. Only mediating the self-identical, indivisible being and the becoming, dividual matter through a third component enables the emergence of the world-soul. This mediation of opposites explicitly happens with violence in relation to what is different.

Cicero consistently translates division from the Greek with the Latin terms *partes, particulae, partitio* and *partiri*. Here, the word group becomes an indicator for the relation of domination of the one over the many, for the violent adaptation of the "other that is hard to mix" to what is the same, the subordination of the divisible under the indivisible. Following the same procedure, becoming is subordinated under being, disorder under order, reasonless perception under thinking oriented to reason.

The process in the foreground of the *Timaeus* passage, however, does not start from partition, but from fusion in the form of violent unification. All things, from the first to the most extreme, things that were previously separated, fuse in the middle and there become one. The middle that Timaeus speaks of is also called *desmós* in 31c, a bond which is all the more beautiful when it "fuses itself and the things which it combines into one." Yet *desmós*, bond, which can also mean shackles and prison in Greek and which Cicero translates with the Latin word for shackles, *vinculum*, indicates the relations of violence that are proper to this middle. Thus, in the *Timaeus* passage that concludes the process of fusing the divisible and the indivisible, Plato emphasizes the government of the one:

καὶ τρία λαβὼν αὐτὰ ὄντα συνεκεράσατο εἰς μίαν πάντα ἰδέαν, τὴν θατέρου φύσιν δύσμεικτον οὖσαν εἰς ταὐτὸν συναρμόττων βίᾳ (Plat. Tim. 35a). "He took the three, as they were, and fused them into one form, adapting by force the nature of the other that is hard to mix to the same."

Following this taming mediation, fusion, unification of the other into the same, a manic process of *partitio*, of partition and distribution, is set into motion in a rampantly complex arithmetic of Pythagorean intervals. In order to bring the divisible-many under the rule of the indivisible-one through the procedure of partitioning, the most diverse and bizarre operations become necessary: the creator god first takes a part from the whole, then takes double the first part as the second part, as the third part one and a half times the second part, double the second part as the fourth part, three times the third part as the fifth part, eight times the first as the sixth part, twenty-seven times the first part as the seventh. This procedure is followed by a series of even more complex operations, which create intervals in multiple dimensions and treat them in various ways. This partitioning functions in a thoroughly regular way, attempting to drive out multiplicity and its restless rumbling in the depths of partition, trying to establish a regulated form of multitude, eliminating everything that is fuzzy, diffuse, obscure. How fascinating a desire to push the sublation of the fleeting difference towards a unified end with no remainder, meticulously dismembering and reuniting the territory of the one in the creation of a numerical structure of the world-soul.

Gilbert de Poitiers. DIVIDUUM, Subsistence, Similarity

Yet another, final beginning would be that with god. In the early Christian discussions of late antiquity and the early Middle Ages, an aspect of theology shifted into the center of attention, which cast new light on questions of relating wholes and parts or unity and multitude. Between Tertullian's dogmatic prescriptions in the early third century and Gilbert de Poitiers' seminal early Scholastic interpretations of the theological tracts by Boethius in the middle of the twelfth century, there was a complex heterogenesis of positions on the question of the trinity and simultaneous unity of the Christian god. More than nine centuries after the first persecutions of heresies and recurrent disputes over the interpretation of the concept of person for the trinity, bishop Gilbert de Poitiers' endeavors to differentiate person, individual and singularity led him into a similarly suspicious situation between self-obscuring writing and ecclesiastical court persecution. *dividuum* plays a role in this.

The doctrine of the three persons in one god, which was formulated in the councils of Nicea (325) and Constantinople (381) so that it seemed to be unequivocal and binding, implied and produced a significant need for discussion, dissensions and orgies of exclusion, both before and after the two councils. The central question was how belief in the one and only Christian god could be reconciled with talk of god as father, son and spirit. Disagreement arose again and again around conceptual solutions that would neither subsume the trinity completely in the one nor allow the unity to be understood as a distribution into three.

Oikonomia appears here, too, specifically as god's plan of salvation and its execution in the history of salvation. The early economy of salvation understood god the father as origin and goal of creation, eternal and uncreated, and son (conceived and yet eternal and outside of time) and spirit as executors. This economy of salvation is found in its most characteristic description around 213 in Tertullian's *Adversus Praxean*: there are three, not according to status, substance or power, but three according to the respective gradation, the respective formation, the respective shaping. In Tertullian's vivid image the father is the source, the son is the river, the spirit is the irrigation canal—the *one* substance for all three is water.

The formulations of the various versions of division, the question of the correct term for the one, and the discussions of the terms *hypóstasis, substantia, ousía, essentia* were marked not only by different theological positions, but also by complex translation problems between Greek and Latin. Along with the diachronous relation between Plato's *Timaeus* (which was to influence all subsequent ideas of creation, for example), Cicero's translation of it, and the fourth century adaptation of the Latin terminology he introduced, a problem of synchronous differentiation also arose during this period. Greek was spoken in the east of the Roman Empire, Latin in the west. Terminological and translation problems conjoined with social situations and theological-political problems, giving rise to serious terminological shifts and parallel genealogical lines that would diverge from one another. The formulation *una substantia* introduced by Tertullian, with which the unity of the Trinity was emphasized, for instance, became problematic when the divine substance was literally translated back into the Greek east with the term *hypóstasis*, because in Greek this implied the diametrically opposite: the personal aspects of the trinity of father, son, and spirit. In mostly futile endeavors to resolve these terminological complications, the doctrines were in part rephrased in new terms; under specific temporal and spatial conditions, central terms such as *ousía* and *hypóstasis* were altogether prohibited and censored in order to prevent misunderstandings. At the same time, in the middle of the fourth century, talk of the three *prósopa* (in Latin *personae*) arose, which was intended to prevent the three hypostases from being understood as three gods.

Modalism, condemned in the third century as heresy, gave rise to the idea that father, son and spirit were only different modes of being, modes of the one god. A similar problem arose when the three persons were, as with Tertullian, only argued in grammatical terms, or only differentiated by name, as a nominally but not actually existing triad. This resulted in the discussion of the fine difference of *ousía*, that father and son are not different in their being, *heteroúsios*, but also not—as it was still formulated at the Council of Nicea—the same, *homoúsios*, but rather *homoioúsios*, similar in their being. Whereas *homoúsios*, as identical, signifies the complete essential identity of father, son, and spirit, *homoioúsios* implies sameness in the sense of same kind, thus not necessarily identical: the son conceived by the father is not of the same being, but rather of the same kind of being.

The neo-Nicean solutions, which ultimately became orthodox doctrine, advocated the solution *mia ousia—treis hypóstaseis*: the father possesses divine being without cause, the son through conception from the father, the spirit by proceeding from the father. In this logic, time is a category of creation. God is not subjected to it in any of his hypostases. His eternity is not a prelude to temporality, nor a continuation after the end of times; it envelops time from all sides. There is no ranking in eternity, but also no time. The causation of the son by the father is completely timeless.

Possible terms to avoid the ambiguity of *ousía* and *hypóstasis* were *una essentia*, linguistically the direct Latin translation of the

Greek *ousía*, and its three *personae*. This concept of person must not be confused with the modern word tied to human beings, but it also goes beyond the old Greek concept of *prósopon*, meaning mask or theatrical role. The one god does not have different masks or slip into different roles. The three persons of the trinity are true persons (*tres personae verae*), actually existing, discrete and complete persons.

Against the backdrop of his wide-ranging translation work from Greek into Latin, Boethius developed around the turn of the fifth to the sixth century his technique of interpreting Christian dogmas with the help of Aristotelian logic. He was therefore influential in terms of the transfer, and thus new invention, of philosophical terms in Latin (with his concept of accidents, for instance). But above all he made a subsequent impact on medieval theological-philosophical discussions and their pre-decisions for modern philosophical discourses that reached beyond theology.

Boethius derived his concept of the individual from Aristotelian logic, as "first substance" and as a certain, physically intended single thing of the sensually perceivable world, which can be, for instance, color, animal or human. However, he conjoined the concept of the individual developed from Aristotelian philosophy with the understanding of personhood that was developed in the Christian-Neoplatonic discussion of the fourth century. In addition to his philosophical writings and scholarly textbooks, Boethius also wrote five smaller theological tracts, the *opuscula sacra*. In one of these tracts, *Contra Eutychen et Nestorium*, he first explains that the person is based on nature, that it cannot be founded on accidents and that it is neither in non-living bodies nor in that which is without understanding and reason. Boethius' concept of person thus excludes non-animate things and animals, but includes humans, angels and god. Boethius thus defined the person—and this definition was to remain in effect for a long time—as "individual

substance of a rational nature": *Persona est rationalis naturae indi-*
vidua substantia (Boeth., CEutN, 3). The Latin *persona*, according
to Boethius' etymological derivation, may come from *sonus*
("sound"), which refers to the necessarily stronger sound that the
actors must produce through the openings of the mask, when they
"represent the people in the comedies and tragedies that these are
about." The mask of the Greek actor, *prósopon*, enables the depiction
of "persons" as gods or humans, "who are certainly recognized
according to their proper form." Yet for Boethius, the translation
prósopon–persona does not capture the sense as well as the translation
of person as hypostasis, as individual substance of a rational nature.

This interpretation of the person is, of course, still marked by
the theory of the trinity and the problem of arguing the one god and
his threeness. In his central theological writing, *De Trinitate*,
Boethius describes this threeness as being "without number":

> *hoc vere unum in quo nullus numerus, nullum in eo aliud*
> *praeterquam id quod est. [...] Nulla igitur in eo diversitas, nulla ex*
> *diversitate pluralitas, nulla ex accidentibus multitudo atque idcirco*
> *nec numerus* (Boeth. De Trin. 2). "This is truly the one, in which
> there is no number, nothing else is in him than that which is. [...]
> In him [god] there is no diversity, no plurality coming from diver-
> sity, no multitude coming from accidents, and therefore no
> number."

According to Boethius, what characterizes the Christian god is that,
on the one hand, he has no cause and does not exist through anything else, but solely that which is. On the other hand, in him there
is no diversity, therefore no plurality, no accidents, therefore no
multitude, and above all no number, and this is so in a specific
sense: Boethius maintains that there are two aspects of the number,

one being the number by which we count, and the other the number that persists in countable things. Whereas the repetition of the number through which we count effects plurality, the repetition of the number in countable things effects no numerous diversity, but rather the repeated predication of unity. When the name of god is spoken three times, the repeated predication thus implies no multiplicity (Boeth. De Trin. 3).

From this reasoning of the trinity in one of two different forms of repetition, which describes god as being without number and as threeness at the same time, Boethius argues (De Trin. 5–6) the trinity as a specific form of relation. He says that the relation does not change or reduce a thing or add anything to it, but rather "holds itself in some way in comparison" (*in comparatione aliquo modo se habere*). In this way, the relation effects that the threeness of god does not imply a differentness of things, *res*, but rather of the divine *personae*. These three persons are not distinguished by being in different places—as different bodies, for instance. Their numerity, their threeness, their *trinitas* in *unitas* is solely a predication of their placeless relation.

Gilbert de la Porrée (Gilbertus Porretanus), born between 1070 and 1080, died 1154, was a theologian, philosopher and bishop of Poitiers.[13] He developed a specific terminology oriented around the Aristotelian categories and Neoplatonic theory, which attained considerable conceptual originality in its further elaboration of Greek philosophy, not only via its reception in early Christian literature, and its transfer into early Scholastic theology. The pinnacle of his theory consisted in the emphasis of singularity, concretion and immanence of all that "subsists," all of that which is. In the midst of an era marked by the dispute over universals, for Gilbert there is no universality in the secular realm, only the primacy of singularity, which comprises not only all that subsists, but also all subsistences.

Gilbert's "doctrine" spread through the influence of his "pupils" around the middle of the twelfth century into a small geography of subsequent impact; like other early Scholastic theologians, however, Gilbert and his work faded into obscurity particularly through the dominance of Thomas Aquinas and the High Scholastic writings. Yet there were also theological and inner-ecclesiastical conflicts that made things difficult for Gilbert during his lifetime and obstructed the reception of his works.[14] At the instigation of Bernard de Clairvaux, he was accused of heresy before the Papal consistory of Paris 1147 and before a further consistory following the Synod of Reims in 1148. Unlike his contemporary Abelard, who was punished with monastery imprisonment and lifelong silence in 1141 due to Bernard's accusations, Gilbert was able to escape condemnation during his lifetime.

An essential reason for this non-condemnation probably lay in Gilbert's multiple caution. First of all, his language was obviously not easy to understand, even for scholars of his day, especially due to the extremely dry and strictly logical ductus of his works, which was unfamiliar for his contemporaries. In addition, Gilbert also authored no explicitly independent writings of his own. He worked mostly in oral form through sermons and lectures. In written form he made use of the genre of the commentary, specifically commentaries on Boethius, to whose *opuscula sacra* he applied detailed interpretations in the 1140s. The genre of the commentary allowed Gilbert to use Boethius' philosophical authority and to go far beyond the texts his commentaries were based on at the same time. Gilbert himself did not claim the position of authorship, but rather that of reading, rendering and interpreting. However, the extensive commentaries on the small theological works by Boethius are in parts ten times as extensive as the commented texts themselves. To this extent Gilbert is an autonomous commentator, who precisely selects what he elaborates and what he just touches upon.

Gilbert's procedure is formally remarkable as well: he incorporates the components of the original text, sometimes only a word, sometimes half a sentence, without exception and in their entirety as building blocks of his own text in his writing, thus artfully developing his own questions and theorems, usually close to the original text. What mostly interests him, though, are the gaps in the commented Boethius texts, which attempt to evade difficulties or release new problems six hundred years after they were written. These omissions are fruitful starting points for extensive problematizations on Gilbert's part. One could say that in the seemingly marginal and servile genre of the comment, he found a specific technique of dividual writing, which turned commenting into an inventive practice.

When apparently purely theological questions were addressed in the early twelfth century, such as the unity of the trinity or christology, these were very concrete questions of legitimizing or questioning ecclesiastical and secular relations of domination. Exactly these dangerous border zones are the spaces of operation of Gilbert's theoretical work. His differentiation of singularity, individual and person is only to be understood against the backdrop of renewed disputes over the concept of person in the Early Scholastic theories of the trinity and in light of the traps of these discourses. This game of truth encompassed finely chased formulations intended to avoid the minefield between unification and differentiation of the divine threeness, an active distancing from heretical genealogies, and the detailed categorization of heretical deceptions.

To understand Gilbert's theoretical position, it is first necessary to emphasize his fundamental decision to make a sharp analytical distinction between the *theologicae rationes* and the *naturalium rationes*. According to Gilbert, the approaches, the *rationes* of the divine-theological realm and those of the secular-natural realm are completely independent from one another and cannot be linked in any way by analogy (Gilb. De Trin. 1, 2, 41). Whereas Boethius introduced a third perspective of equal value between the other two, the *mathematicae rationes*, the way Gilbert develops his theory is almost consistently strictly dual. Without any mediation, without interim stages, without blurring instances of correlation or analogy, theological and secular perspectives are strictly opposed. The two different modes of being, the divine *essentia* and the secular *subsistentia*, correspond to the two different perspectives *theologicae rationes* and *naturalium rationes*.

On the basis of this sharp separation, another distinction, transversal to the first, is significant for Gilbert, which he introduces following Boethius: the distinction between *quo est*, "through which something is," and *quod est*, "what something is." This distinction applies to the divine as well as to the natural realm, but it is expressed differently in the two realms and in different terminology.

For the *naturalium rationes* Gilbert uses a pair of terms newly posited in this meaning, by shifting Boethius' conceptual schema: *quo est* is called subsistence (*subsistentia*), *quod est* is called the subsisting (*subsistens*). The term *subsistentia* had been used for various meanings since Marius Victorinus in the third century, but the relationality of subsistences and subsistings is Gilbert's own invention. Unlike the pair substance (essence) and accidents ("inessential" characteristics), which was introduced by Aristotle and which became established in Latin through Boethius' translations of the Aristotelian theory of categories and Porphyry's *Isagoge*, the relation between subsistence and the subsisting is not hierarchically striated, but rather envisioned as a relationship of mutual exchange. Even though the subsisting exists "through" subsistence, it does not develop out of subsistence, but is co-emergent with it. At the same time subsistence exists in it. The subsisting does not emerge as a multiplication from a one. It only exists "through something," but at the same time it is singular, and "its" subsistence (that through which it is) is also singular (Gilb. De Trin. I, prol. 2, 6 and especially I, 5, 23).

In the *theologicae rationes* Gilbert runs into considerable linguistic and also theological difficulties. Here *quo est* means essence (*essentia*), following the old early Christian solution in seeking to avoid the concept of substance. Occasionally Gilbert takes a sidetrack along a different conceptual line and designates the *quo est* of the divine essence as *divinitas* (divinity), the *quod est* of the trinity as three persons of the one *deus* (god). Here the *quo est* remains an absolute unity, whereas the *quod est* assumes an extraordinary, divine form of (persisting, not countable) number. At the same time, the features of the person cannot be explained as accidental or substantial forms, because the one would contradict the simplicity and the other the unity of god. Gilbert is experimenting here on unstable ground: the differentiation between divine essence and god is sufficient reason for suspicions, because the divine essence must be envisioned as a simple unity. Plurality, on the other hand, still belongs to the natural and creaturely realm.

Whereas Gilbert conceptualizes the essence of god as *divinitas* (Gilb. De Trin. I, 2, 36) and form without matter (I, 2, 52), the threeness is described as repetition without difference (I, 3, 7), pure repetition of the name of god as well as of the thing itself. This pure *repetitio* of person without numeration in the divine realm is, as with Boethius, contrasted with that of the natural realm of countable things, whose different properties effect the numerous diverseness of things (I, 3, 10). The theological approach thus yields the opposition between a one without numeration, a numberless, measureless all-one, without beginning and end on the one hand, and a plurality, the *numerus*, which is subject to counting, *numeratio*, on the other.

For the guardians of dogma (especially the Augustinian line of the interpretation of the trinity) affiliated with Bernard de Clairvaux, no less suspicious than the (accused) separation of god and his essence was the fundamental separation of the divine and secular realm. For Gilbert there can be no meeting, no mediation between the two realms. Even in the case of minor deviations, the sharp emphasis on the incommensurability, the opposition, the differentiation of the realms of being and their approaches is conspicuous. Because the two realms cannot be mediated in any way, multiplicity cannot emerge from unity, cannot unfold from it.

To the extent that the radical multiplicity of singular subsistences and subsistings is founded in itself, the hypothesis could be hazarded that Gilbert's world needed neither god nor trinity. What Bernard de Clairvaux considered sufficiently suspicious for an accusation provides us with an opportunity to envision the Gilbertian realm of the secular as strictly immanent, multitude not as lack, but rather as molecular multiplicity relieved of the commandment of unity, without god, without trinity, but also without substitutes for transcendence: numberlessness and measurelessness to the many refusing to be counted by the one.

Gilbert's most consequential invention for the history of philosophy was the differentiation of singularity, individuality and personality. Three steps were needed in the development of the doctrine of the trinity, leading from Augustine through Boethius to Gilbert and resulting in very different effects, including with respect to views of the secular realm outside theology. Notwithstanding the six centuries between Boethius and Gilbert, Gilbert is important in this genealogy as a late link in the chain connecting the philosophy of antiquity, the theology of late antiquity and Early Scholasticism. With Augustine, the concept of personality, the three *personae* of the divine essence, was alone at the center. With Boethius, individuality came into play, the concepts of the singular and the individual were used in more or less the same sense. It was not until Gilbert's commentaries on Boethius that singularity assumed a different field of application that was both concise and broader than that of individuality.

In the full differentiation of the three concepts, singularity becomes for Gilbert the conceptual starting point that describes the singular in its broadest extension. Gilbert takes this up in his commentary on the fifth section of Boethius' tract *De Trinitate* when he attempts to more precisely examine *transsumptio*, the translation of the concept of person from the secular to the theological realm, which Gilbert finds problematic. In the fifth section Boethius expounds on the notion that the differentness of the three persons of god is found in their relation. Gilbert uses these theological ideas on the theory of the solely relational, but not numerical threeness of god for a long and wholly independent excursus (I, 5, 20–37). First he expresses skepticism about every form of direct transfer or assumption of the concept of person from the secular to and by the divine. Nevertheless, he finds it necessary to precisely clarify "which of the subsisting is called person in which way" (I, 5, 21). This question about the differentiation of person in the secular realm leads Gilbert to a more precise distinction of three extensions:

Quod ut facilius possit intelligi, illa que superius huic loco distinguenda reservavimus distinguamus: scilicet quod alicuius proprietas alia ratione 'singularis,' alia 'individua,' alia 'personalis' vocatur. Quamvis enim quicquid est individuum, est singulare—et quicquid est persona, est singulare et individuum—non tamen omne singulare est individuum. Nec omne singulare vel individuum est persona (Gilb. De Trin. I, 5, 22). "To make it easier to understand, we now want to distinguish what was reserved for distinction above: depending on the various approaches, a property of something is called 'singular,' 'individual' or 'personal,' because everything that is individual is singular, and everything that is a person is singular and individual, but not everything that is singular is individual, and not everything that is singular or individual is a person."

With this differentiation Gilbert introduces a distinction along various extensions: the smallest extent is attributed to personality, the middle extent to individuality, the greatest to singularity. However, this differentiation of extensions does not correspond to a hierarchization or graduation, nor in any way to a relationship of unifying or unfolding the one from the other. This is a distinction at the level of conceptual extension: the individual comprises a greater area than the person; the singular in turn comprises the individual and the person and more.

A precondition for Gilbert's thinking is that none of the three concepts has to refer solely to human beings. Nor does Gilbert, in his rigidly logical method, follow Boethius' influential reduction, according to which a person is the indivisible substance only of rational nature, so that it applies to god, the angels and human beings. Gilbert also explicitly rejects the philosophical use of the concept in Boethius' *Contra Eutychen et Nestorium*. Unlike the legal meaning in antiquity, Gilbert's concept of *persona* does not differentiate human beings from one another as those who are persons *sui iuris* and as others (such as women, children, and slaves, who can be assigned to the realm of things according to patriarchal Roman law), nor does he differentiate human beings as creatures of reason on the one side and animals and plants on the other (Gilb. De Trin. I, 5, 33: "any living creature and any tree and endlessly many of this kind").

Without following this specific line of exclusion, Gilbert's concept of person is nevertheless smaller in its extension than that of individuality and of singularity. For Gilbert, *persona* is quite generally the name of a part of the subsisting that are individuals. Using the popular etymology that *persona* developed from *per se una*, "for itself one," Gilbert defines *persona* primarily as "entirely for oneself," "nothing that is other than itself" (Gilb. De Trin. I, 5, 29–37). Gilbert only pursues this line of personality, however, after a detour that is conceptually extremely productive. In the course of this, he concentrates mostly on differentiating the two further extensions, individuality and singularity.

Three centuries before the purported discovery of the individual in the Renaissance, a clear idea emerges in Gilbert's commentary of how the conceptual definition of the individual is to be situated: individuality arranges all subsistences found in or at a single thing into a whole. The specific feature of this "individual" ordering mode of individual singularity is that all singular subsistences of a thing are united according to exactly the formation in which it is concretized. In order to designate, found, "make" "one" (singular) thing, subsistence is needed. For "this one and whole" (individual) thing, additional properties are needed that are not caused by accidents, but which become visible, "adapted," "tested" through them. Individuality implies a unified orientation of all the substances and accidents belonging to this one and whole thing, also in time: the individual arrangement applies to all parts of the whole that "were, are, or will be" (I, 5, 25). At the same time, individuality cuts the connection with other (co-forming) subsistences in other things. Its crucial components are exclusion of similarity and of co-formity, dissimilarity, and wholeness as closure.

However, there is also another ordering mode of singularity, a transversal mode that transversally collects the singular elements in a twofold way and without consideration of their belonging to an individual formation. This form of collection is neither unification nor generalization (the process terms *collectio* and *unio* are used here, but not *unitas*), it crosses right through the areas of the single things as subsistings and subsistences. For this second, doubly transversal mode of singularization, Gilbert finds a concept, which he places next to the individual. It is not universals, generality or community that are posited opposite individuality here, but the term *dividuum*. With this Gilbert describes a non-individual singularity, which is not distinguished by the properties of individuality—wholeness and dissimilarity. The concise "invention" of the term *dividuum* can thus certainly be attributed to Gilbert, who writes in the relevant passage (Gilb. De Trin. I, 5, 23–24):

> *In naturalibus enim quicquid est, alio, quam ipsum sit, aliquid est. Et quoniam id, quo est aliquid, singulare est, id quoque, quod eo est aliquid, singulare est. Nam plura numero sicut uno singulari non sunt aliquid ita unum aliquid sine numero esse non possunt. Itaque singularitate eius, quo est, singulare est etiam id quod eo aliquid est. Sepe autem diversa numero singularia secundum aliqua eorum, quibus sunt, conformia sunt. Ideoque non modo illa, que sunt, verum etiam illa, quibus conformia sunt, unum dividuum sunt. Ac per hoc neutrum illorum, quibus conformia sunt illa que sunt, individuum est. Si enim dividuum facit similitudo, consequens est, ut individuum faciat dissimilitudo.* "In the secular realm, everything that is something is something through something else other than itself. And because that, through which something is [subsistence], is singular, that which is something through it [the subsisting], is also singular.[15] What is plural according to number cannot be something through one singular, just as it cannot be one without number. Therefore, through the singularity of the subsistence, the subsisting is also singular. Often, however, singulars that are diverse according to number

are co-forming according to their subsistences. Hence, not only the subsistings, but also the subsistences through which they are co-forming, are unum dividuum. And that is why no subsistences, through which the subsisting are conform, are individual. If similarity thus makes dividuum, dissimilarity consequently makes individuum."

Not exactly simple, these sentences contain in nuce an entire theory of dividuum and its conceptual components.

1. Dividuality as Dispersion

As the name says, dividuality first means "dividedness," "divisibility," although oddly enough not in relation to a whole. In the narrower sense of the word there is already a connotation of "dispersedness." Dividuality implies not (only) the dividedness of entire single things, but rather an extension, a distribution which moves, scatters, disperses, spreads through diverse single things.

Even though *dividuum* is in diverse single things, it does not one-sidedly stand opposite the *individuum* as a universal. It is one of Gilbert's terms that break through the dichotomy of the individual and the universal, introducing a new dimension in which the parts of a non-whole are posited in a non-hierarchical, transversal relation. Even though it would seem to suggest itself at the peak of the dispute over universals, *dividuum* is definitely not a universal. The dividual abstraction is no universalizing separation, separatedness, disjunction from the concrete, but rather an abstraction as a conjunctive disjunction. The dividual emerges in dispersion, in the transversal distribution, in drawing the abstract line that traverses and concatenates the concrete single things. The line is abstract to the extent that it detaches and affirms parts from the individual-holistic concretion. The line of abstraction is the non-whole *unum* in *unum dividuum*. On it and with it and in it, the separated subsistences and subsistings, dispersed and distributed to diverse individuals, assemble.

2. Singular Subsistence, Singular Subsisting

Gilbert purposely chooses two very close terms, *subsistentia* and *subsistens* (of which the neutral plural is also *subsistentia*), when he seeks to conceptually grasp the close, complex and non-hierarchical inner-worldly connection between that through which something is and that which is. The subsisting *is* through the same subsistence that inheres to it, that is in it. Subsistence is the principle that effects the concretion of the subsisting, yet not like a universal ground, but rather as the respectively specific and singular subsistence of a respectively singular, co-emergent subsisting. A subsisting single thing does not have its being from an outside, but rather from the subsistence that is in it. Conversely, a subsistence is not in diverse subsistings, but only in one. A single subsistence "makes" only one single subsisting thing.

The distinction between subsistence and subsisting is not at all analogous to that between *dividuum* and *individuum*. Gilbert emphasizes: "… not only the subsistings, but also the subsistences […] are *unum dividuum*." Dividuality applies to both aspects, to the multiplicity of immanent-causal subsistences and to the multiplicity of concrescent subsistings. This twofold multiplicity does not start from a unity, nor does it dissolve into a unity. Instead, it multiplies itself in the abstract lines that simultaneously separate and con-catenate the concrete.

3. Similarity and Co-Formity

The individual is a whole that can be identified in space and time, a one which is composed in a specific way; it is individual through the complete fullness of its substantial and accidental properties, a fullness that divides nothing. As Gilbert emphasizes, its property is *dissimilitudo*, dissimilarity. In contrast, what literally distinguishes dividuality is *similitudo*, similarity. Not whole, not same, not unified, but divided, similar, co-forming. Whereas individuality mobilizes dissimilarity to emphasize the respective being-different, demarcation from everything else, dividual singularity is always one among others. *dividuum* has one component or multiple components, which constitute it as divisible and concatenate it with other parts that are similar in their components: similarity, not sameness or identity, similarity concerning only some components. Whereas the concept of individuality tends toward constructing closure, dividual singularity emphasizes similarity in diverse single things, and thus also the potentiality of connecting, appending, concatenating.

Gilbert is not concerned with the relation of similarity between creator and creation; here too he does not integrate the two realms of the divine and the natural. Unlike the theological perspective of the divine that understands the relationship between the persons of the trinity as a relation and a simple *repetitio* beyond counting, dividual similarity in the secular is based on a complex transversality of single things and their forms. *unum dividuum* is that which is, and that through which it is—not simply something, but also "co-forming." The Latin *conformitas* is not to be understood as the word "conformity" is used today in the sense of a moral designation of compliance. Instead, co-formity tends to a particular form of diverseness. Gilbert writes in De Trin. I, 1, 12 *quamvis conformes tamen diversas—immo quia conformes ergo numero diversas*: as is explicit in Gilbert's rather uneven formulation, something is "co-forming, not only although, but because it is diverse in number," singular and manifold. Diversity and conformity are not to be seen as mutually exclusive, but rather as mutually conditional.

Co-formity means that parts that share their form with others assemble along the dividual line. Dividuality emerges as assemblage of co-formity to form-multiplicity. The dividual type of singularity runs through various single things according to their similar properties. Co-formity implies the dividual alignment of parts and parts co-forming with them in other single things, an alignment toward a specific resonance, not toward a unison form, but toward the sharing of formal components. This co-formity, multi-formity, constitutes the dividual parts as *unum dividuum*.

II. DIVISION

[: Ritornello 4: Sand, Castle, Sea, Line :]

[: *A child* in the expanse, *gripped with fear, comforts* itself by drawing a line in the sand. It divides the expanse of the beach with its line. From time to time it runs out of breath, is drawn further by the line, stumbles along, *as best it can*, behind its line. The line is *like a rough sketch of a calming and stabilizing center in the heart of chaos. Perhaps the child skips* as it follows the line, but the line *itself is already a skip*: it is not straight, it is irregular, bends, drops out and continues again. It divides the chaos, *jumps from chaos to the beginnings of order in chaos, and* it is *in danger* of being erased, of dissolving, of *breaking apart at any moment.*

Attracted by the even more immeasurable expanse of the other, external element, the child and its line are drawn to the water. To appease the *forces of chaos, keep them outside*, the child tames the line, makes a strong curve at the shore and continues drawing the line, until it becomes a circle. Closing the circle results in a small and yet generous territory. The child uses the earth that has been dug up to build a wall on the inside of the moat. Wall and moat protect against the sea flooding in, which constantly approaches from below. And others come, and the child builds gates and opens them, *lets someone in* and participate in its creation, many someones, walking *in a circle as in a children's dance.*

The child and its many more begin to build the castle, and the chaos of the sea once desired becomes more and more of a danger. *This involves an activity of selection, elimination and extraction, in order to prevent the interior forces of the earth from being submerged, to enable them to resist or even to take something from chaos across the* gates and sluices *of the space that has been drawn.* First the rough contours become recognizable. A mighty hill is formed, and then on top of it the first fortifications, jagged and edged. More and more details mark the emergence of the castle, fine gradations, posts at various heights, watchtowers, inner and outer circles with different equipment. And the child partitions the many, to ensure the order of maintenance and repairs with clearly assigned tasks. *A mistake in speed, rhythm or harmony would be catastrophic because it would bring back the forces of chaos, destroying both creator and creation.* :]

Partition, Participation, Division

Partition, participation, and division are not three successive movements in a linear history or three circumstances that can be completely separated, but rather three modes of a single thing. They can be imagined as overlapping, can be opposed to one another, jumbled, their order can be reversed.

The first mode is that of partition. This is the mode of separation, of striating time and space, of attributing and distributing the parts. In the mode of partition the parts are assigned to appropriate places, functional positions, rightful owners. Partition is the attribution of the parts, which has limitation both as goal and as effect. It starts from a certain order, in which time and space are pre-structured, to newly reproduce order again and again. Implicit and explicit regulations, instructions, laws hold the parts in their position, in their separation and limitation under an autochthonic *nomos*. Every territory that comes into view is measured and identified as something to be partitioned. Partition is a distribution of the shares, a distribution according to ownership. The mode of partition is a procedure of counting and measuring, producing equivalence and quantifiability. It cuts the parts off from everything they are capable of. It inhibits the concatenation of the parts. In partition, being-divided becomes being-unconcatenated, being suspended and yet dependent.

The second mode is that of participation. It is the procedure of organic partaking. The whole is its starting point and its goal. The basic schema of participation can be described with Boethius' theological tract *De bonorum hebdomade,* on which Gilbert de Poitiers also wrote a commentary. In the third and sixth introductory axioms of the tract, Boethius explains the difference in participation between that which is being and that which simply is and thus participates in being:

> III. *Quod est participare aliquo potest, sed ipsum esse nullo modo aliquo participat. Fit enim participatio cum aliquid iam est; est autem aliquid, cum esse susceperit.* "What is can participate in something, but being itself participates in no way in something. Participation happens namely when something already is; but it is something when it has received being."

The precondition "when something already is" indicates the difference: being can (and must) participate in nothing, because it is beyond participation. It enables participation, but is external to it.

> VI. *Omne quod est participat eo quod est esse ut sit; alio vero participat aliquid sit. Ac per hoc id quod est participat eo quod est esse ut sit; est vero ut participet alio quolibet.* "Everything that is, participates in that which being is, in order to be; it participates in another, however, in order to be something. And thus that which is participates, in order to be, in that which is being; it is, however, in order to participate in something else."

Here too, Gilbert de Poitiers' deviation from what he has to comment on is notable. Gilbert interprets both of Boethius' axioms on participation as inner-worldly participation with the help of his concepts of subsistence and subsisting: no subsistence that is in a subsisting participates in anything in any way. That subsistence, unlike the subsisting, participates in nothing also means that it has no quality or quantity whatsoever. Conversely, the participation of the subsisting means that it has properties and size (Gilb. DHeb I, 38–42). Whereas for Boethius, being, in which everything that is participates, is presented as all-one, for Gilbert every singular subsisting participates in "its" singular subsistence (Gilb. DHeb I, 55: *omne subsistens participat eo quod est eius esse*).

When Gilbert has to explain the relation between divine essence and created world, he points out the fundamental difference between the theological and the worldly realm: whereas in the world, every having is itself already participation, in the realm of essence (which does not have to participate, because it is being itself) Gilbert speaks of an *extrinseca participatio* (De Trin I, 2, 45). Beyond participation, which is entirely external to it, is the principle of being, which communicates with all otherness with the help of "external participation."

Organic partaking means the constant production of a whole. It does not mean tearing apart a whole, tearing it into pieces, parting it into parts independent of one another, but rather entering into a certain social relation of wholeness, being its part and thus reproducing the whole. The parts operate like organs as dependent functions of an organism. That is the organic logic of the whole, the community, the totality. *Partem capere*, taking the part, partaking. This sounds like active taking-share, even offensively capturing a part. Yet participation is never primary, it follows the whole. And the whole is not to be had. The par-taking of participation implies a retrospectively having of a part. First there is the whole, a share of which is taken, in order to newly produce it. The part stays related to the whole and governs itself in reference to the whole. Contrary to partition, participation does not operate through separation and classification. The *partes* of participation are linked to one another through their reference to the whole, they require exchange and intercourse with one another under the auspices of the whole, for which they become subservient, compliant. *communio*, holy community. Logic of relating to the whole, constant reference, subordinating the part under the whole.

The third mode is that of division. Here, division is not a mathematical operation, which divides an existing whole into equal parts. It is not limitation and classification like partition, and it is not participation, not partaking as a subserving relationality, as a permanent reference to a totality, to an encompassing whole. Instead, division divides and consolidates indeterminate-diffuse multiplicity. This multiplicity must be understood neither as a preceding nor as a future whole; it is a field of immanence, in which divisions draw their lines.

The mode of division is re-singularization. In dividing it posits a singularity, which detaches itself from the manifold and affirms it at the same time. Division takes its measure from multiplicity, it is a specific measure that engenders singular unambiguity in multiplicity. Division is the selection of a line, it chooses a line. It is the Platonic procedure of dividing.[1]

Plato's dialogue *The Statesman* is not only a fundamental writing on the *politiké techne*, modes of governing and constitutional forms of the Greek *polis*. It also offers implicit demonstration and manifold instructions in the Platonic method of division. Division, *diairesis*, is not a momentary positing, but rather a long and winding path. Plato's *atrapos* (258c), the way, the line, which is to lead to a clear idea of the most suitable statesman, is itself not necessarily straight. In a contorted and sometimes erratic way, the dialogue pursues the question of how, from the multitude of insights and their different fields of applicability, a figure can be chosen which appears to be most suitable for the task, the technique, the art of governing.

Even though there are no unified rules for the procedure of division, *The Statesman* provides several explicit guidelines for its application. Dividing serves to distinguish ideas, and this is best done by clearly cutting through (*témnein*): "it is not safe to whittle off shavings; it is safer to proceed by cutting through the middle!" (262b) A division into humans and animals, for instance, or into Hellenes and barbarians is wrong, because this does not cover the distinction between species and part (262–263). A division into as few parts as possible is described as the best division: if dividing into two is impossible, then division must be carried out into the next smallest number of parts possible (287c). Further advice regarding good division is not to think of it from the end: "Let us, then, not make our division as we did before, with a view to the end, nor in a hurry, with the idea that we may thus reach political science quickly" (264a). Division is best carried out with open-ended results and without a perspective of a too narrowly defined *télos*, without fear of detours, accepting dead ends, patiently testing further.

Yet in terms of open-ended results the strongest image of division in *The Statesman*, the process of purifying gold, leads in the opposite direction: it is fairly untypical not to have the end in sight when extracting gold. On this Plato says:

> "The refiners first remove earth and stones and all that sort of thing; and after that there remain the precious substances which are mixed with the gold and akin to it and can be removed only by fire— copper and silver and sometimes adamant. These are removed by the difficult processes of smelting and refining, leaving before our eyes what is called unalloyed gold in all its purity." (303d/e)

Extracting gold certainly has pure gold in view, so this seems to contradict the methodological demands of not looking towards the end and not simply pursuing it in a straight line. Here, however, Plato is aiming at something else. He uses the image of the gradated mixture and separation, con- and disjunction, repeated smelting and refining, mainly to emphasize that the procedure of division is all the more difficult and tedious, the further it has progressed. Related territories, neighboring zones, similarities require greater efforts of division than the first, rougher distinctions of division.

The schema of Platonic division is well rendered in the image of attaining gold: "Let us then leave one half and take up the other, and then let us divide that entire half into two parts." (261c) Division seems to follow its path as a chain of distinctions, as a multi-stage selection, as far as possible to the end of the *atomon eidos*, a no longer separable and divisible concept that has no sub-concepts. Yet this movement of specifying a concept from the greater species to the next smaller one is only superficially at the center of the Platonic procedure. Through the seemingly rigid chain of distinctions, the multiplicity of possibilities always shines through. When Plato addresses the question of the best herdsman for the herd of human beings in *The Statesman*, there is a whole series of candidates to be carefully distinguished: merchants, farmers, food-makers, trainers, physicians, helmsmen, then those hired for wages, heralds, those who deal with divination, priests, finally orators, generals, judges. And this does not exclude the possibility that there may be endlessly many other candidates. It remains open whether new, surprising candidates may be found beyond the next curve in the line, traversing the identifications of singular occupational groups. Indefinite multiplicity is the precondition and constant companion of division, and heterogenesis is affirmed and re-singularized in the chosen path, in the singular line, no matter how discontinuous it may be.

This is not the Aristotelian form of dividing a genus into opposite species. It does not specify, but instead selects against the backdrop of a multitude of selectable lines, which may be chosen from a diffuse multiplicity. Division is not partition, that is, classification and distribution as domination, and it is not participation, relating the parts to the whole. It is not the dissociation into one or the other species against the backdrop of a given genus. Categories, genera, species are not further distinguished. Dividing rather means selecting a singular line from manifold material.

Drawing a line is not an identification. Because it operates in an unlimited field of consistency, the singular division cannot have a unifying effect at all. It tests, it divides, it posits, but it does not close. Nor does it want to get rid of the surroundings of the division, but rather to actualize, newly situate, streak them in the procedure of dividing. The line is a chain of affective-intellectual, social-machinic positings, of detours, breaks, hesitations, changes of direction, turnings, warps, new connections—it is multiply broken, leaping, hopping, never the shortest path from a to b. Choosing a line never erases the multiplicity it comes from.

Dividing means positing *one* line, no unification, but also no duification. In the Platonic procedure, the drawing of the line is itself foregrounded, not the duality, not the ambivalence that emerges through bisection, folding or bifurcation, nor the in-between of two points. The line is not drawn *between* two points, but rather the division affirms the one line of many, producing singular unambiguity.

But can it really be said that the choice of line does not erase the multiplicity that it comes from? In the progression of division in *The Statesman*, it seems as though this procedure increasingly cuts off parts, eliminates them. For Plato division is undoubtedly (and wholly contrary to the later understanding of *divisio* as classification into conceptual pyramids, especially in the Scholasticism of the twelfth and thirteenth centuries) a moody procedure, unpredictable in its movement, its breaks and leaps. In the state of undecidedness and uncertain end, it is also easy to underscore the incompliancy of Platonic division. And yet with Plato, what is wild is always already on the way to domestication: gold wants to be purified, the most suitable statesman/*politikos* wants to finally be nominated, and the line of flight will have turned into a lineage that has always been certain of its genealogy.

In *The Statesman*, however, there is a remarkable, small empowerment to envision the wild, and it appears in the form of a dismissal. It takes us *ex negativo* to the traces of a form of subjectivation that Platonic statesmanship does *not* cover, cannot cover or does not want to cover. This form adds something to the false division that envisions the end as a whole from the perspective of this very end and falls back into the logic of participation. Here, in this added value, division is transformed into a potential of dividuality, which does not need to reduce the line to lineage, but instead turns it into an irregular and overflowing stream.

Close to the beginning of the dialogue, following the division into the inanimate and the animate, into the "apsychic" and the "empsychic," statesmanship is attributed to the living, because "the king's art is not, like that of the architect, one which supervises lifeless objects; it is a nobler art, since it exercises its power among living beings and in relation to them alone" (261c). The next cut is also relevant for us and is intended to divide the animate, the empsychic, the living once again: the care of the *politikos* is not for the breeding and nurturing of singulars, but for the common (*koinos*), the herds (*agele*) (261d). The *monotrophia*, the "feeding of the one," the care of a specific life, turning to the singular, is expressly not a matter of the statesman. In the summarizing preliminary definition as well, this is how the function of the *politiké techne* is described: the art of governing is "the art which we said gave its own orders and had to do with living beings, but had charge of them not singly but in common" (275c). Whereas governing the common is the realm of statesmanship, the singular life of singularities is beyond its interest.

In a further passage, where the topic is taken up again, the argument gains clarity in our sense, as the division into community and singulars is shifted to *tithasoi/hémeroi* (tamed/human beings) and *agrioi* (wild): "For if their nature admits of domestication they are called tame; if it does not, they are called wild." (264a) This escalation of the classification into commonly (= human) and singly (= wild) living beings indicates a more general governing technique of inclusion and exclusion. Here the herd of the tamed is the enclosed, enclosing and bounded totality, the collective subject of statesmanship, which draws along with it the exclusion of the single wild beings, the incompliant, the unteachable. In this idea of the *politikos*, the herd is thus, first of all, not comprehensive and, secondly, not interested in singulars.

It is up to us to reverse the reading of the ungovernable in this conception of statesmanship, to affirm this figure rather than exclude it, to insist on its immanence: there are ways of living that as *agrioi* elude the statesmanship of the *politikos*, which do not allow themselves to be tamed, are not compliant with his care. Incompliant, ill-bred, untamed, they do not want to belong to the community of the governed, but want to live under the motto of division as single, divided, separated, not drawing their lines in the enclosed and enclosing terrain of the herd, but rather in the field of immanence of multiplicity, right through the participative arrangements of the parts and their partitive striation. This "wildness" is not grounded on a relation of inside and outside. The incompliance of the "wild ones," the sheer possibility of not complying, also reverberates in the terrain of the community. And the fact that these non-compliants live as singulars, but not unified, communalized, herded, does not necessarily discredit every possibility of their concatenation.

Community. *munus* as Minus

The problems of the terms affiliated with *communitas/Gemein-schaft* emerge before and beyond their very resonance with totalitarian communities, *Ur-* and *Volksgemeinschaften*, also before and beyond the problematic dichotomy of individual and community: on the one hand they cling to identitarian forms of composition, on the other they remain bound to the mode of reduction, subtraction, diminution. And even where both aspects are dialectically conjoined,[2] they remain on this side of communion. The entire conceptual line of the commune, the community, the common,[3] even communism itself, to the extent that dogma and pressure to confess have been and are practiced in its name, are thus cast in the dubious light of a double genealogy of identitarianism and reduction.

In addition to the extensive literature on questions of community in the field of communitarism theories, in the 1980s and 1990s a number of authors from the leftist spectrum of political philosophy also became interested in the concept of community. The titles of their texts not only contain the terms *communauté, communità, communitas*, but also further differentiate these terms with various adjectives. Jean-Luc Nancy (1983, 2001), Maurice Blanchot (1983) or Giorgio Agamben's (1990) minor works on the inoperable, the confronted, the unavowable or the coming community are probably the most well-known examples of this tendency.

In the tradition of ancient Rome and the etymology of *com-munitas*, as well as in the tradition of Christian community between communion and (early) Christian community, there are two repeatedly recurring problematic aspects. One is well known and has often been discussed: the community as a term for an identitarian mode of closure, protection and simultaneous exclusion, basis and ground for a heterosexual, patriarchal gender order as well. The other, less illuminated side of *communitas* relates to the question of the obligatory bond that binds the singulars to the community.

The first problem can be well summarized with the words of Jean-Luc Nancy, the French philosopher who wrote two short but, for this discourse, highly influential texts for this discourse about the "inoperable" and the "confronted community." In the second text, published in 2001, Nancy critically distanced himself from his first text of 1983—critically distancing himself altogether from the use of the term *communauté*, community—with several sentences that could hardly be more explicit:

> Little by little I have preferred replacing it [the word 'community'] with the awkward expressions *being-together, being-in-common*, and finally *being-with*. [...] I could see from all sides the dangers aroused by the use of the word community: its resonance fully invincible and even bloated with substance and interiority; its reference inevitably Christian (as in spiritual, fraternal, communal community); or more broadly religious (as in Jewish community, community of prayers, community of believers or *umma*) as it is used to support an array of so-called ethnicities. All this could only be a warning. It was clear that the emphasis placed on this necessary but still insufficiently clarified concept was at least, at this time, on par with the revival of communitarian trends that could be fascistic."[4]

This is the clearly expressed dissociation of one of the authors, who in some contemporary discourses continue to be misunderstood as proponents of the philosophy of community.

The second question of the obligatory bond that binds the singulars to the community is closely tied to the first problem of communion as identization, uniformization, closure. The Latin term *communitas* is derived from the prefix *con-* for "with," "together," and the noun *munus*. *munus* first of all means a gift. In Republican Roman use, however, there are to a lesser extent indications of gifts in the sense of a voluntary exchange, and rather of the moral/economic obligation to sacral duties, personal service (such as in the form of military service) and the payment of financial fees as "tax obligation." Here *munus* assumes a mainly obligatory meaning. The obligation of rendering the most diverse kinds of services and fees is understood as a debt in both a moral and economic sense. The *munus* constitutes the community as co-obligation, and it is the reason for the acceptance of the individual into the community based on a relation of duty and debt. For this reason, in her historical, etymological and political theoretical analysis of *munus* and *communitas*, Isabell Lorey speaks of a "logic of tribute, levy (*Ab-gabe*)," which in Roman law was by no means based on equality.[5]

So even from a historical and etymological perspective, it could be said that the diminution aspect of the concept of community is an essential component of its use. In this respect, community can never be understood as surplus, as multiplying division, as alliance and gain. Rather, the logic of debt and obligation results in limiting singularity, in giving over, giving up oneself.[6] Community is grounded on sacrifice and debt, relinquishment, rendering, surrendering. The band, the binding, the bond decreases singular capabilities. In the desire to become more, community implies becoming less. The *munus* is a minus.

The Desire for Self-Division

> And if thy right eye offend thee, pluck it out, and cast it from thee: for it is profitable for thee that one of thy members should perish, and not that thy whole body should be cast into hell. And if thy right hand offend thee, cut it off, and cast if from thee: for it is profitable for thee that one of thy members should perish, and not that thy whole body should be cast into hell. (Mt 5:29–30)

Jesus sits on the mountain holding his first great speech. It is an invocation to charity, developed from the stern commandments of the Old Testament, a fulfillment of these commands, at the same time a new beginning. In place of the threat of retaliation, Jesus stakes the claim to offer yet the other cheek. This is the extreme morality of charity: in concrete terms of the eye, the command is no longer "an eye for an eye," but rather "pluck it out and cast it from thee." This is by no means a dilution of the severity of the Old Testament, but rather a radicalizing escalation: from revenge, from punishing justice, from the retaliation of violence for violence to self-injury, self-dismemberment, *self-division*.

"That there is something great in self-denial, and not only in revenge, must have been inculcated into man only through long habituation [...]." So Friedrich Nietzsche interpreted self-division in the winter of 1876/77 in an aphorism from *Human, All Too Human* (I.3.138) as a component of centuries of training through Christian morality. The self-sacrifice relieves both god and man, who "grasps the spears of his enemies and buries them in his own breast." "Breaking oneself into pieces" is actually to be understood as "a very high degree of vanity": "The entire morality of the Sermon on the Mount belongs here: man takes a real delight in violating himself with excessive claims, afterwards idolizing this tyrannically demanding something in his soul. In every ascetic morality man worships a part of himself as God and for that he needs to diabolize the other part." (I.3.137) Most of all, it is the logic of confession that leads people to internalize division, to cross over from subjugation to a double mode of subjectivation as self-glorification and self-subjugation. And this transition is only possible as the division of the self appears together with a desire, a desire that affects individuals, seizes them, invokes them

1. Moral Unity

Human, All Too Human is Nietzsche's first larger treatise on morality, starting from a critique of anthropocentrism, which places "moral man" all too humanly as ever the same, "sure measure of things" (I.1.2.) at the center. The "moral man" presupposes himself as precondition: "what he has essentially at heart must also constitute the essence and heart of things" (I.1.4). Nietzsche calls the second main section of the first volume "History of Moral Sensations." In this section he develops a sequence of various stages of *Christian* morality, but also its most important components, such as moral unity, moral substance, moral community, or the moral individual. "Moral sensations"—as Nietzsche already clarifies in the first main section—are "rivers with a hundred sources and tributaries" (I.1.14). They are manifold complexes, which can always also allow other sentiments to resonate with them. Morality, i.e. with Nietzsche mainly Christian morality, is what makes these moral sensations, which are resonating and consonant, but not at all in unison, still appear as unity. It is Christian morality that first unifies the multiplicity of moral sensations into a unified moral edifice: "Here too, as so often, the unity of the word is no guarantee of the unity of the thing." (I.1.14) The thing itself, the manifold moral sensations are a multitude, divided, and then unified into a unity through the constant normalizing stream of pastoral government.[7]

2. Moral Substance

Even more, the Christian discourses of morality envision and engender not only a "unity of the thing," but imagine also its substantial immutability. Nietzsche derides the "purblind mole's eyes" that "never see anything but the same thing," always the same, immutable, unconditional substances. In defense of the mole: although the animal may be nearly blind, it is certainly capable of distinguishing substances in their quality and their mutability. Reducing the multiplicities to a unified and always same substance is not due to the capacity of sight, but rather to Christian dogma and its ideological successors, which are not willing to allow views other than the timelessness of divine substance. In this respect, Nietzsche is also willing to recognize a constant of the original error in matters of free will and belief in same substances that is almost meta-historical and not limited to Christianity: "It may even be that the original belief of everything organic was from the very beginning that all the rest of the world is one and unmoving." (I.1.18) Against this kind of construction of substance and immutability, Nietzsche posits the radical processuality of morality and its continual becoming: "Everything in the domain of morality has become and is changeable, unsteady, everything is in flux [...]" (I.2.107).

3. Moral Community

"To be moral, to act in accordance with custom, to be ethical means to practice obedience towards a law or tradition established from of old." (I.2.96) Nietzsche the philologist adheres fairly strictly to the etymology of morals from the Latin *mores*. The *mos* as law, which is based more on a tradition than on agreement in producing a concrete universal, already indicates the necessary condition of internalizing morality. Yet where does this obedience come from, this "being tied to a tradition, law"? Nietzsche connects tradition above all back to the "preservation of a community, a people." To maintain the community, law is needed as tradition, as convention, as custom, and it must be unconditionally accepted by each individual: "a community of individuals likewise compels each separate individual to observe the same custom." (I.2.97) Unlike the Platonic notion of the government of a community by the statesman in opposition to the singulars as its outside, Christian morality is interested *a priori* in a comprehensive government of the whole and the singulars. *Omnes et singulatim*. Breaking loose from the lineage of customs is "dangerous, and even more injurious to the community than to the individual." The older the tradition is, the more its origin has been forgotten, the more reverence is due to it, until it finally becomes holy, becomes "the morality of piety."

Yet, there is also a twofold prehistory of good and evil, a classification of goods and their internal hierarchization and graduation (I.2.42). Morality is introduced on the one hand as a structure of the "community of the good," as the firm ground of "ruling tribes and castes." It is on this ground that good and bad are distinguished, that this distinction between good and bad is produced, that something like "common feeling" can emerge—from the outset, as it were, as a criterion of gratitude, revenge, and exclusion, through which individuals are mutually interwoven and obligated. Because those who are bad are powerless and cannot requite, as "a swarm of subject, powerless people," a mass "like grains of sand," they stand opposite the powerful.

This layered arrangement of castes, well ordered through both the sympathy and hostility of those who are good, and the power-lessness of those who are bad, is countered from the perspective of the subjected and powerless by a wild confusion: "Here every other man is, whether he be noble or base, counted as inimical, ruthless, cruel, cunning, ready to take advantage." Human beings are per-ceived as fundamentally evil, unsuitable for communization in their separation, and thus their doom is imminent. What is con-ceptualized in Plato's *The Statesman* as a dual image of a community of the governable and its opposite, single wild beings, is presented by Nietzsche in a more complex way, as a double perspective of a common that, seen from above, incorporates its opposite, the powerless, and appears, seen from below, as an unordered, raw assemblage not capable of community (I.2.45).

4. The Moral Individual

As one of the many constitutive fallacies from the world of morality, Nietzsche also problematizes the individual, showing how, with a little imagination, it could lose its totality and identity on the axis of time. Nietzsche emphasizes the aspect of temporal change and with it the constructedness of an unalterable character and the unal-terability of the individual altogether. An unalterable character seems only possible due to the fact "that during the brief lifetime of a man, the effective motives are unable to scratch deeply enough to erase the imprinted script of many millennia." Tying into this, Nietzsche's mental exercise consists of imagining that an 80,000-

year-old man would have to comprise an abundance of different individuals evolving out of him one after another and demonstrating "a character totally alterable" (I.2.41). Multiple individuals in one human being: this is the reversal of Gilbert de Poitiers' temporal interpretation of the individual, in which the individual also comprises its past and future: Gilbert's idea of the order of the individual applies to all parts of the whole, specifically those that "were, are, or will be" (Gilb. De Trin. I, 5, 25). This order addresses the genealogy of the individual as much as its subsequent impact, beyond its physical status as living or dead. The opposite interpretations of the temporal extension of the individual with Gilbert and Nietzsche both show, in their own ways, the limitations of a moral determination of the individual character.

In *The Three Phases of Morality Hitherto* (I.2.94), Nietzsche describes the development of morality in three sections, in the first of which man's actions are no longer directed "to the procurement of momentary wellbeing but to enduring wellbeing," thus becoming attuned to utility and purpose; then he surrenders himself to common sensations and regulates his conduct upon the basis of honor, and finally, in the "the highest phase of morality hitherto," he becomes the lawgiver to opinion: "he lives and acts as a collective-individual." There is a correlation between the subordination of the individual and the development of a strong community based on similar, characterful individuals.

Against this backdrop, in the following aphorism 95 on the *Morality of the Mature Individual*, Nietzsche emphatically posits the strictly personal, amoral action against the impersonal, which stands as a mark of the moral action of the "collective-individual." To "make of oneself a complete *person*" means foremost not to labor for one's fellow men because of "pity-filled agitations and actions," but—wholly in keeping with the individual-anarchistic tradition of

Max Stirner—only to the extent "that we discover our own highest advantage in this work: no more, no less." In the Preface to "free spirits," Nietzsche already speaks of a great disengagement, which enables unbinding oneself from the strongest binds, breaking free from unbreakable bonds. For Nietzsche, the strongest bond is moral obligation, *Angebinde*, the bindings of reverence to the traditionally honored and the "gratitude to the soil out of which they have grown." In contrast to this, like an earthquake, "a licentious, vulcanic desire awakens for wanderings, going abroad, alienation." (I.Preface.3). Such a social jolt is more likely to be expected from the "more unfettered, uncertain and morally weaker individuals," from "men who attempt new things and, in general, many things," than from "firm-charactered individuals." (I.5.224)

Nietzsche's amoral and disengaged individuals are "distinct single and unique human beings" (I.5.283). Max Stirner conceptualized the "Ego" as unique, but not necessarily as an isolated individual, rather in its "intercourse," against the people, against the state, against society, against common welfare, in short against everything general, yet still on the basis of an idea that "self-enjoyment" also has something to do with "intercourse." Where and how the isolated individual becomes the singular ego, the moral individual becomes the free spirit, cannot be precisely determined, neither in Stirner's nor in Nietzsche's writing.

5. The Moral *dividuum*

For Nietzsche, morality is the "self-division of man"—as aphorism 57 is entitled. The examples listed for this logic of dividing the self always feature a desire for self-splitting, but under the conditions of the pastorally governed individual (of the nineteenth century) and its highly gendered specificities. Nietzsche, for instance, imagines an author who desires to be obliterated by another author, "presenting the same subject with greater clarity and resolving all the questions contained in it," or a girl in love who "wishes the faithfulness and devotion of her love could be tested by the faithlessness of the man she loves," or the soldier who "wishes he could fall on the battlefield for his victorious fatherland," or the mother who gives her child the sleep that she deprives herself of, also her food, her health, her strength, if need be. (I.2.57) All of these examples are examples of desire, not of coercion; although they are paradoxical, or perhaps even perverted, they are nevertheless not coerced.

Nietzsche does not consider these examples in the moral logic of selflessness simply as "unegoistic states," but rather conditioned by the way "that in all these instances man loves *something of himself*, an idea, a desire, an offspring, more than *something else of himself*, that he thus *divides* his nature and sacrifices one part of it to the other." Sacrificing the offensive member is intended to save the whole. The desire for division arises neither from selflessness nor from compulsion. The "moral man" voluntarily divides his individual wholeness—presupposed as such—and sacrifices one part to another. No external compulsion, but an affection for something engenders this self-division.

Nietzsche's aphorism on morality as division of the self marks the first pronounced appearance of the concept *dividuum* in modernity, and it presents itself, as it were, as a central component of morality. Nietzsche concludes the aphorism on self-division with the sentence: "In morality man treats himself not as individuum but as dividuum."

What does it mean that a human being considers themselves not as indivisible, but rather as divisible? What does it mean that the possibility of the dividual appears alongside the naturalized self-understanding as individual? Beyond Nietzsche and his opposition of the model of a "mature individual" and that of the self-dividing *dividuum*, this pair can certainly be considered compatible in the paradigm of pastoral government. The individual is produced in morality, invoked as undivided and indivisible, and urged all the more to "self-division." Individuation and dividuation are thus not at all as opposite as it seems. At this point they are instead two strategies of pastoral power that complement one another: the production of individuals goes hand in hand with their (self-)division.[8]

6. Morality and Subjection

At first there seems to be only the alternative of subjection or a dangerous, great disengagement from morality. Yet it is already clear to Nietzsche that there are at least two modes of subjection, namely "whether one subjects oneself with effort or gladly and willingly" (I.2.96). These two modes of subjection do not emerge separately, but are related to one another, and they are also subject to the changing movement from one to the other. One of these movements consists in becoming accustomed to subjection to tradition, to customs: "But one does perceive that all customs, even the harshest, grow milder and more pleasant in the course of time, and that even the strictest mode of life can become habitual and thus a source of pleasure." (I.2.97)

Through habituation, normalization and naturalization, "free/voluntary obedience" [*freier Gehorsam*] emerges from compulsion and pure subjection: "Morality is preceded by compulsion, indeed it is for a time itself still compulsion, to which one accommodates oneself for the avoidance of what one regards as unpleasurable. Later it becomes custom, later still voluntary obedience, finally almost instinct: then, like all that has for a long time been habitual and natural, it is associated with pleasure [...]"

(I.2.97). It is not only the threat of the isolated individual being excluded from the community, but rather a mechanism of inclusion and self-division that determines pastoral power. The pastoral structure of morality is increasingly less based on governing through repression than on the production of the free/voluntary obedience of individuals, on the instructions for the voluntary and "self-determined" division of the self, at the same time on a desire that yearns for and induces this self-division.

As co-editor of the French edition of Nietzsche, Michel Foucault did not remain untouched by Nietzsche's reflections on the functions of morality and asceticism in Christianity.[9] While he was able to start from the proto-poststructuralist positions that can already be found with Nietzsche, he expanded these in the lectures and books of the last years of his life into extensive historical and philological investigations. First in modernity, then in the Middle Ages, then in Antiquity, he elaborates foremost those aspects of morality that extend beyond elements of repression and concern the specific modes of subjectivation, self-care and self-government. These practices of morality are characterized by a movement that is already anticipated in the peculiar conjunction of freedom and obedience in Nietzsche's concept of *freier Gehorsam*.

In the second volume of *The History of Sexuality*, Foucault explicitly describes his theoretical thrust, how he was led to "substitute a history of ethical problematizations based on practices of the self, for a history of systems of morality based, hypothetically, on interdictions."[10] Nietzsche also did not consider morality to be one-sidedly determined by law and subjection, but proposed a scale of morality between compulsion and desire; yet what still appears in his writing to be a development from compulsion through free/voluntary obedience to instinct, as a movement from repression and compulsion to subjection to desiring self-division, appears in Foucault's writing as simultaneous and inseparable components of pastoral power in the form of codes of behavior and modes of subjectivation.

> In short, for an action to be 'moral,' it must not be reducible to an act or a series of acts conforming to a rule, a law, or a value. Of course all moral action involves a relationship with the reality in which it is carried out, and a relationship with the code to which it refers, but it also implies a certain relationship with the self. The latter is not simply 'self-awareness' but self-formation as an 'ethical subject,' a process in which the individual delimits that part of himself that will form the object of his moral practice, defines his position relative to the precept he will follow, and decides on a certain mode of being that will serve as his moral goal. And this requires him to act upon himself, to monitor, test, improve, and transform himself.[11]

Self-formation as a moral subject goes far beyond noting a constructedness of the subject structured by morality. Self-formation as a moral subject means the continuous modulation of the self, which as a mode of subjectivation recursively affects the codes of behavior as well. But self-formation also indicates the increasing weight of dividual-machinic components. Alongside the forms of codified morality, ethico-aesthetic practices of the self take hold in a contradictory process. Over and above the mode of subjugation to a moral state apparatus, machinic subservience effuses the self-governing service of social and technical machines. Despite all critique of moral humanism, Nietzsche's perspective remains centered on the individual; the dividual seems to be a peculiar, particular case. Yet it is the individual that is produced and revised in and by pastoral power, and at the same time, it proves to be self-governing, self-dividing,

self-deifying and demonizing, self-taming in free/voluntary obedience, in the compliant practices of a self that modulates itself and
its assemblages. As an antidote, Nietzsche also has good advice for
Kafka several aphorisms earlier: "One may well want to look out
over the topmost rung of the ladder, but one ought not to want to
stand on it." (HATH, I.1.20) Climb several rungs back, to the stem
of the blade, into the middle between the "roots of the world" and
the fragrant, intoxicating "blossom of the world" (HATH, I.1.29),
in other words back to where one can be swept along by the things
and their molecular dimensions.

Schizos. Subsistential De/Foundations of Dividing

"Five pence for one—two pence for two," says the sheep to Alice behind the looking glass. The one egg is more than twice as expensive as two eggs, not because it is a particularly precious egg named Humpty Dumpty, but because one must always be more expensive than two. This invocation of oneness is useless, though, because the old nursery rhyme knows all too well how the story will end: "All the King's horses and all the King's men, Couldn't put Humpty together again." The whole cannot be arranged again by the King's horses, or by his men, but not because it is something especially fragile that can only be repaired with great difficulty, if at all. It was always already divided, crumbling, manifold.

Schizos are erroneously regarded as split personalities. Yet multiplicity is not cleavage. They are not split, but manifold. The split indicates a whole that has been severed. In contrast, schizos traverse strata and perforate the skin of the individual. In their subsistential territories they look around themselves and into other milieus. Right through the striation of the parts arranged by partition and domination, athwart the arranged whole of community and participation, they attempt to keep an open view of the expanse of immanence. By no means only projections of heroizing psychosis and schizophrenia, schizo-lines are omnipresent, in all kinds of seemingly deviant commonplace gestures, in daydreams, in accidental poetic formulations, in tripping over one's own feet, in traffic jams, everywhere where a child of any age jumps out of its circle and draws a line, a tangle that cannot be shaped into a whole, despite all normalization, self-government and machinic subservience.

"In short, we have an already shattered Humpty Dumpty who cannot be put together again …," wrote Ronald D. Laing in the late 1950s in the introduction to his book on *The Divided Self.* In these early critical psychiatric studies, Laing already noted that schizoids do not simply have a split ego, but rather experience different kinds of division, cracks in their relationship to their world. Although Laing attests them a high degree of vulnerability, his thesis is based on a more general disposition of "ontological insecurity." The sovereign individual is supposed to see him or herself as intact, certain, whole, one, but it is not only the reality of the schizoids that looks different. A life without certainties feels torn, sometimes more dead than alive. Yet it is less a withdrawal, a retreat from the world that surrounds one. "Living in a world of one's own" does not mean so much the separation of the schizoid from the world, but that "the world of his experience comes to be one he can no longer share with other people."[12]

Despite the social contextualization, however, Laing tends to reduce his concept of "ontological insecurity." In his phenomenologically influenced investigation, he falls back on interpretations in which all sociality requires the centrality of the individual, and "real relationships" require "being alone with oneself." Yet the concept of ontological insecurity implicitly indicates a different perspective, one that shifts the focus from the individual (and the individual's complement, society) to modes of socialization and subjectivation. With Judith Butler, this shifted relation can be described as fundamental dependency, vulnerability, exposure. In her book *Precarious Lives*, published in 2003 (and in several further texts up to the present), Butler develops a version of "ontological insecurity" that goes substantially further, envisioning vulnerability and insecurity starting from the social. "Loss and vulnerability seem to follow from our being socially constituted bodies, attached to others, at risk of losing those attachments, exposed to others, at risk of violence by virtue of that exposure."[13] With this shift from individuality to sociality Butler also insists that this vulnerability is always differently expressed. It is not merely a characteristic or temporary state of a certain person, it does not bear on primarily one or another individual body, but on the middle of bodies as an asymmetrical relation, as radically differently endangered sociality.

In *State of Insecurity. Government of the Precarious* (2015), Isabell Lorey proposes a concept of "precariousness"[14] which, in analytical distinction to "precarity" and "governmental precarization," also emphasizes the fundamentally irreversible, social dimension of the precarious: "it is always relational and therefore shared *with* other precarious lives. Precariousness designates something that is existentially shared, an endangerment of bodies that is ineluctable and hence not to be secured, not only because they are mortal, but specifically because they are social."[15] So the insecurity in Laing's concept of "ontological insecurity" cannot be simply transformed into security, physical or mental. The asymmetries that permeate all power relations can be changed, but not fundamentally eliminated. There is no "return" to before the condition of precariousness.

In the philosophy of antiquity, this problem was treated even more fundamentally as a question of the mortality of bodies, of dividuality: everything that has a body is divisible, *dividuum*, dissoluble, and hence mortal. This was how Cicero argued the academic critique of the Stoic notion of the essence of the gods in his third book on *De natura deorum*, which questioned the transience of living beings, and thus the corporeality of the gods:

> *corpus autem inmortale nullum esse, ne individuum quidem nec, quod*
> *dirimi distrahive non possit; [...] Ergo itidem, si omne animal secari ac*

dividi potest, nullum est eorum individuum, nullum aeternum; atqui omne animal ad accipiendam vim externam et ferundam paratum est; mortale igitur omne animal et dissolubile et dividuum sit necesse est. (Cic. Nat. deor. 3,29) "but no body is immortal, nor indivisible, nor of the kind that cannot be separated or torn apart. [...] when all living being can be cut up and divided, then none of them are indivisible, none eternal. Yet every living being is amenable to assuming and accepting an external power. Thus every living being must necessarily be mortal, dissoluble, and divisible [*dividuum*]."

Every living being is divisible, every division threatens its life and indicates its mortality. And as Butler and Lorey emphasize vulnerability and precariousness, and so the dimension of precarious life, precariousness extends not only beyond the individual, irreversibly and ineluctably social, but also beyond the circle of human beings. Not only human bonds form the endangered basis of life, but also the relationships of all living creatures.

To further expand these ideas, I would like to move from ontological insecurity through precariousness to arrive at a concept of subsistential division inspired by Gilbert. I write *subsistential*, because I think that concepts like ontological or existential are too closely tied to notions of the unified and antecedent essences of a ground, a cause, a *quo est*. The multiple Gilbertian concept of subsistence, on the other hand, enables considering each singular subsisting in relation to "its" respectively singular subsistence, and not to a unified essence, an immutable substance, a universal. The subsistential territories, the subsistential de/foundations of dividing imply an asymmetrical intercourse, which is not necessarily an exchange, not a measuring and adapting of the parts, but also not a tribute in the sense of cutting off a part (the minus of the *munus*) as precondition for coherent individuation and unified community.

In a relatively traditional manner, the "case studies" and conclusions by the young Ronald D. Laing in *The Divided Self* are still oriented to establishing wholeness, identity, substance, and psychical cohesion, in order to expect from this a linear progression to the normalization of sociality. The "case" of the chemist James exemplifies this specific striation, which applies to alternative psychiatry as well. Clearly situated in the chapter on so-called "petrification and depersonalization," the man is described as being lightweighted, substanceless, and therefore uncertain. Asserting that James makes his mother responsible for his lack of identity, Laing identifies James' wife as having "a forceful personality and a mind of her own," and James dreamed of hanging onto her body like a clam.

> Just because he could dream thus, he had the more need to keep her at bay by contriving to see her as no more than a machine. [...] She was an 'it,' because everything she did was a predictable, determined response. He would, for instance, tell her (it) an ordinary funny joke and when she (it) laughed this indicated her (its) entirely conditioned, robot-like nature, which he saw indeed in much the same terms as certain psychiatric theories would use to account for all human actions.[16]

Envisioning the dividual machinization of social relationships as individual petrification is marked by the hierarchy of the therapeutic situation, by profound gender stereotypes, but also by the classically humanist preconception that the human person stands at the center of all relations.[17] Yet the fact that James wants to append to the body of his wife like a clam, that he and she communicate with one another in machinic form, also still leaves room for other interpretations. It is not necessarily a matter of keeping a "strong woman" at bay, but perhaps exactly the opposite, a specific form of making machinic contact between monadic components. In the clam image, clinging to the woman's body without a split or self-division attains a quality of maintaining some autonomy, while appending to the machine at the same time.

The marvelous turn in Laing's story is that the invention of a machine is mirrored in the anthropocentric glasses of the therapist himself. At the point where the machinization leads James to refute and reject other positions, to having his own views, reaching a "certain measure of autonomy," Laing himself also becomes part of the machine:

> However, it became evident that his apparent capacity to act as an autonomous person with me was due to his secret manoeuvre of regarding me not as a live human being, a person in my own right with my own selfhood, but as a sort of robot interpreting device to which he fed input and which after a quick commutation came out with a verbal message to him.[18]

Laing interprets the machinization of relationships as depersonalization and objectification. Yet becoming-machine does not simply depersonalize the one or the other part of communication, it depersonalizes the entire relationship. It is not "totally disarming the enemy," nor the voiding of "personal aliveness" by objectification as an appendage, but the desire to attach to the machine, the appending to the machine that drives the clam-machinist. "With this secret outlook on me as a thing he could appear as a 'person'. What he could not sustain was a person-to-person relationship experienced as such."[19] Indeed, it is not a matter of a "person-to-person" relationship on the basis of two wholly indivisible individuals. Machinic individuation evades the personalization of individuality and the individualization of singularity; it works in a dividual way.

[: Ritornello 5: Drawing the Line Again :]

[: *Finally, one opens the circle a crack, opens it all the way, or else goes out oneself.* One lets it become a line again and *launches forth. One opens the circle not on the side where the old forces of chaos press against it but in another region, one created by the circle itself.* The line is newly drawn, *as a function of the working forces it shelters.* Following the guidance of a line, one *launches forth* from the castle, is drawn out, *hazards an improvisation. Along sonorous, gestural, motor lines that mark the customary path of a child and graft themselves onto or begin to bud "lines of drift" with different loops, knots, speeds, movements, gestures, and sonorities.* :]

III. DIVIDEND

[: Ritornello 6: A Thousand Machines :]

[: *The narrative of man's becoming-machine as a purely technical alteration misses the machinic, both in its civilization-critical development and in its euphoric tendency. It is no longer a matter of confronting man and machine to estimate possible or impossible correspondences, extensions and substitutions of the one or the other, of ever new relationships of similarity and metaphorical relations between humans and machines, but rather of concatenations, of how man becomes a piece with the machine or with other things in order to constitute a machine. The "other things" may be animals, tools, other people, statements, signs or desires, but they only become machine in a process of exchange, not in the paradigm of substitution. According to Guattari, the primary characteristic of the machine is the flowing of its components: every extension or substitution would be communicationlessness, and the quality of the machine is exactly the opposite, namely that of communication, of exchange. Contrary to the structure, which tends toward closure, the machinic corresponds to a tendentially permanent praxis of connection.*

Machinic subservience, conducting modes of subjectivation beyond social subjection, is the governmental shadow-side of the potentiality even of advanced means of communication. The de-pendency on machines is multiplied in the continuous ap-pending to, sus-pending from the machines, being-pendant on the machines. The high art of machinic subservience interlocks a permanent online life with the imperative of life-long learning and the irresolvable merging of business deals and affects. The streams of desire of the ubiquitous appendages generate new forms of dependency, which make the material penetration of the technical machine into the human body appear as a secondary horror scenario. And yet, the desiring machines are not simply tools of machinic subservience; the minor advantages of the resistive use of new abstract and diffuse machines in dispersion are by no means always already over-coded.

Concatenations of chainless machines, bound together by the lack of any bond. :]

Capitalism and Machine

Machinic capitalism does not signify a new phase of capitalism, a new "age of the machine," a further link in the sequence of industrial and post-industrial, fordist and postfordist capitalism or liberalism and neoliberalism. The machinic is a category that accompanies and traverses capitalism in its diverse instantiations, also helpful for distinguishing these historically different forms. From Mary Shelley's *Frankenstein* through the Marxian machine fragment to the appendix of *Anti-Oedipus*, ever new interpretations of the machinic appear, but not in such a way that humans determine technical apparatuses or apparatuses determine humans. The machinic changes with the mutations of capitalism, adapts, deforms itself, and forms its surroundings at the same time.

In his "Postscript on the Societies of Control," Gilles Deleuze explains these mutations of machine and capitalism as an arrangement in three phases: the societies of sovereignty combine levers, pulleys and clocks with the sovereign government of subjects, the disciplinary societies combine energetic apparatuses with the enclosure of subjects, and the societies of control operate with "machines of a third type"[1] and modes of subjectivation that may more than ever be called machinic subservience. This schema is not to be understood as a linear, techno-determinist or even teleological sequence, but rather as an irregular accumulation of diverse kinds of societies, which overlap today and modulate the machinic in ever new ways with the most recent developments of logistics and algorithmics, of data collection and data browsing, of social media and financial derivatives.

"Self-driving cars" are certainly technical apparatuses, but mainly they are machines. In the tautological formulation of the self-driving auto-mobile there is an almost desperate insistence on the magical possibility of self-movement. Most of all, though, it is the exchange, the communication, the connection through (data) streams, (data) traffic, which machinizes the relation of body-machines, thing-machines, and social machines, also in street traffic. People will still have the feeling of sovereignly steering (for example, when they enter one of the four-and-a-half destinations that they, on average, aim to reach daily), but at the same time, within machinic tracking everything steers and conforms itself, regardless of whether thing, human or social intercourse: no more enclosure, but self-conduct of all components in an open milieu, which move past one another as elegantly as possible and, depending on the identification of the individual thing (from the license plate of the car through the machinic facial recognition of those in it, to the mass movements of diverse vehicles), comply with a multiplicity of openings and closures.

The concept of machinic capitalism,[2] which does not indicate a new phase of capitalism, but an increasing significance of the machinic in contemporary capitalism, does not imply a further version of the dichotomous preference given to objects (over subjects), animals (over humans), materialities (over the immaterial), realisms (over discourses). Rather, it concerns the flows passing through these dichotomies and through the single things—data flows, currents, desires, becomings, middles, dancing relations, the in-between of dividual sociality.

Becoming-machine of the devices, apparatuses, equipment: when technical apparatuses come into play, they are never only technical apparatuses, but foremost components of machinic intercourse. In this respect the notion of the machine invading the human being is already wrong: cardiac or brain pacemakers, for example, are more than technical apparatuses, non-human alien elements that turn the human being into a machine, an electronic tag is more than a substitute for prison walls, chips for locating animals are more than the dog leashes of the control society. Human enhancement is more than the improvement of human beings by technical artifacts, prostheses, implants, neural interfaces, operations, and substances. In all of these examples the machinic is not simply a means used by humans, but a specific relation, first of all a relation of appending.

In many situations it appears as though machines were not penetrating into human beings as much as humans are being drawn "into the machine." I am not only dependent on a "machine" external to me, which surveils and subordinates me, I also want to become part of the machine, append to it. In this sense, machinic subservience is entirely different from subjugation to the machine. The pull of machines, their attraction, has undoubtedly led to new, very bodily desires, to relations of appending, streaking, and enveloping. Material size plays no role in this: regardless of whether it is a small mobile telephone or the extended facilities of the NSA—all that is relevant is appending to the networks, the clouds, the machines. Appending to the machine also means being dependent on the machine. The desire to be online, for instance, has aspects of being permanently reachable, Internet addiction, and apparatus fetishism at the same time. Yet the latter is more than just a means of distinction, compulsion to consume, or simply the desire for the latest devices and gadgets. There is also an urge for increasingly strong haptic techniques of streaking, swiping, stroking. Swiping across screens, thus streaking screens, simultaneously de- and reterritorializing the screens, this is undoubtedly just as much a new cultural technique as the accelerated thumbs of the smartphone generation. Streaking/swiping the screens also has something of a haptic differentiation that goes far beyond identifying letters in text messages, in email or social media messages on the smartphone. Swiping across the screen not only means streaking the device, gently striating it, but also affectively approaching it, stroking it. To the extent that this ephemeral stroking carries out the same movement in the same place, it corresponds to a reterritorialization. To the extent that it does not stroke the same place twice, but instead scrolls over the surfaces of virtual content, streaking them, stroking over them, it is deterritorialization.

The more the material relation of proximity, the development of appending to the machines is differentiated, the more it appears as though human beings wanted to "get into the machine." Yet "getting into the machine" is a notion similarly false as that of the "machine penetrating into the human." Perhaps it is more of an endless convergence with the technical apparatuses, which endlessly differentiates both material and immaterial intercourse. It is a relatively small step from typing letters on keyboards to swiping across screens, which could be expanded in the future. Verbal control is a potential mode of this expanded assembling, or also using body parts other than fingers and hands. Feet could come into play, for example, as with a sewing machine, a drum, an organ, or a wah-wah pedal, or the whole body—like the sound assemblage of a one-man band, singing with a drum on the back and a tambourine under one foot.

Large desktop touchscreens are taking the place of keyboard operation, and yet notebooks, pads, smartphones are still carried around today, as personal means of production, as fetishes, gadgets. Future machinic environments might be more readily conceived in terms of the logic of enveloping than of appending or physically touching. Whether we want it or not, whether we know it or not, most data is already largely in the clouds. All that is missing then is omnipresent access to the data-pumps that we can plug into anywhere without further mediation, or, one step further: a way of dealing with data clouds that is by no means incorporeal, but imperceptible. Touchscreens drive the development of apparatuses from visible appendage toward an increasingly invisible envelope. Machinic sensors do not necessarily have to work through touching the apparatuses. Gestures, hand signs, body language instead of Google Glass and data gloves. Perhaps the theremin is the instrument of the future. No external, visible envelope that comprehensively envelops everything, but rather an endless (self-) enveloping of every single person, access, at the same time, to the machinic environment, to the extent that the control of the codes allows it.

Ghostly music, glissandi generated without touch, hands and arms gliding through the air, electromagnetic fields moved by the electric vibrations of the body. Gliding, flowing, floating, flying music. Just as Leon Theremin began to play his instrument nearly a hundred years ago, the people of today are beginning to play the technical instruments, the apparatuses, the equipment that surrounds, besieges, envelops them, the environments and surrounds, and they are played by them. There is something of virtuosity at work here on both sides. But as said before, this is not a matter of instrumental relations, of machines as tools and means of human beings or vice versa. We are not playing instruments, but rather playing with them, the way children play with other children, with things and machines.

In the 1970s some children played with remote-controlled cars, boats, and airplanes. These were wonderful tools for teaching especially boys to control machines at an early age. The overkill that was to be avoided in all cases was the removal of the boat/car/airplane from the range of the remote control. Fifty years later it will be a question of keeping all single things, not only apparatuses but also people, within the range of remote control, whether in gaming, in street traffic or in everyday life. Only the remote control is missing, and so is the person who operates it. Just as the auto-mobile does not really move itself, the self-driving car will not drive itself either. Where people once divested themselves of effort, now they are divesting themselves of control. Machinic self-conduct means a complex interplay of various components that comply with and assemble into an assemblage. Self-assembling and assembling the assemblage.

And not only the streets want to be machinically regulated, but airways increasingly also require machinic engagement. With regard to the acquisition of drones, while politics insists almost too conspicuously that drones are controlled by humans, it can be said with Stefano Harney and Fred Moten that "drones are not un-manned to protect American pilots. They are un-manned because they think too fast for American pilots."[3] The dys- and pan-topic fantasy of logistics aims to limit human beings as "controlling agents" as far as possible, to liberate the flow of commodities and weapons from human time and human error. This does not mean that humans become superfluous: to the extent that they survive them, they will continue to have to explain the collateral damage of drones. It is inherent to their "signature strikes" that they are not always completely free from errors. The drone brings death or it brings mail from Amazon, based on algorithmically produced risk or potentiality profiles. Most of all, it promises precision beyond human exactitude. Targeted, smart, reliable, damage-minimizing precision in a machinic environment. The drone is the machinic animal of the present, and at some point it will also unfold itself, multiply itself.

Facebook: Self-Division and Compulsion to Confess

"Facebook enables you to connect with the people in your life and share with them what matters to you."[4]

"One has to be completely taken in by this internal ruse of confession in order to attribute a fundamental role to censorship, to taboos regarding speaking and thinking; one has to have an inverted image of power in order to believe that all these voices which have spoken so long in our civilization—repeating the formidable injunction to tell what one is and what one does, what one recollects and what one has forgotten, what one hides and what hides itself, what one is thinking and what one thinks he is not thinking—are speaking to us of freedom."[5]

In his Sermon on the Mount, Jesus taught machinic subservience and self-compliance, confessional communication and self-division. That is what Facebook *also* is: in addition to being a means for self-presentation, com-munication, and manically showing off one's life, in addition to being a hotspot of future social media bubbles, in addition to being a tool for Facebook and Twitter revolutions, in addition to being an indelible memory of millions, it is also a medium of confession, indeed a compulsion to confession, and in this sense it is a medium not just of com-munication, but also of self-division.

Facebook enables me to further optimize this machinic practice of division. The "formidable injunction" of our civilization to "tell what one is and what one does, what one recollects and what one has forgotten, what one hides and what hides itself, what one is thinking and what one thinks he is not thinking," is in good hands with Facebook. With one limitation: what does not apply, or only under certain conditions, is the external compulsion inherent to the word "injunction." Here everything revolves around machinic subservience, the will to confess, the desire to communicate.

In the first volume of *The History of Sexuality*, using material on medical tests, psychiatric examinations, pedagogical reports and family controls of sexuality in the eighteenth and nineteenth centuries, Foucault describes a new form of power, which is based foremost on various new forms of confession: "it required an exchange of discourses, through questions that extorted admissions, and confidences that went beyond the questions that were asked."[6] Against what Foucault calls the repression hypothesis, he brings the intensity of confession into play, the ineluctable relation of power and pleasure: "Power operated as a mechanism of attraction; it drew out those peculiarities over which it kept watch. Pleasure spread to the power that harried it; power anchored the pleasure it uncovered."[7]

As pastoral power, Christian morality combines the compulsion to confess with the desire to admit. It can refer to a long genealogy of confessional practices since the High Middle Ages. Since these medieval upheavals, power as a mechanism of attraction, a siren call to confession, has multiplied, enticing from all sides, spreading its sounds across all social strata. It not only entices me to relieve myself in confession, but also with the promise that I could decipher my most inner secrets just by making them public:

> The obligation to confess is now relayed through so many different
> points, is so deeply ingrained in us, that we no longer perceive it
> as the effect of a power that constrains us; on the contrary, it

seems to us that truth lodged in our most secret nature, 'demands' only to surface [...].[8]

This is the central statement of Foucault's confession theory. The idea of a truth only waiting "in our most secret nature" to surface, is also the basis for the ubiquitous propaganda of transparency today. Its primary procedure is to connect an identitarian self and its truth that *must* step out of the dark; if this does not succeed, then it can only be because transparency is shackled by a power, a force, a compulsion that it must liberate itself from. Reversal of the perspective to power: instead of seeing a manifold power at work, which operates by invoking confession and permanently producing desires to confess, every kind of power is regarded as a homogeneous block of the potential repression of confession. Confession, in contrast, has a liberating effect from this perspective, it helps to escape from silence, sets truth free. Division here assumes foremost the excessive form of confessional communication and publication. Stolen truth, that which the public has been denied, the de-privatized wants to surface.

Against the backdrop of this appeal to enable the freedom of confession, the private increasingly falls into the defensive. Privacy appears as a concept in the limited meaning of data protection, at most: in the field of social networks, discourses focus on the illegitimate storage of personal data and the impending loss of privacy. Privacy is supposed to provide an answer to the question of how this data may be protected from access by others: protected, first of all, from state repression against single persons, but also from the valorization of the (accumulated) personal data by commercial actors. In light of increasingly excessive state surveillance programs and commercial misuse of personal data, these are problems that need to be taken seriously; at the same time, however, they are barely varied repetitions of the one-sided narratives of decline, which have lamented the decline of either the public or private sphere in ever new combinations. And these narratives often fall below even the level of old science fiction motives of the surveillance society from *1984* or *Brave New World*.

Beyond the data protection discourses, or rather parallel to them, the "internal ruse of confession" gains a new explosiveness. What does it mean when a desire spreads that does not lament the decline of the private sphere at all, but seems instead to flirt with a voluntary abandonment of all privateness? What does it mean when in social media people are not simply forced to convey their data, and this even for the economic ends of others, but when they downright develop a compulsion to de-privatization? Taking the example of Facebook: the problematic aspects of the business model of Facebook lie not only in the exploitation of unpaid labor, in the identification of users for advertising clients, or in the opacity of the privacy policy and the privacy settings of Facebook. The underexposed side of social networking is the desire to publicly communicate oneself, to render (up) one's data, to divide oneself.

This new desire for "self-division" in social media is based on the urge of virtual sociality to surface, an urgent necessity for visibility, which is connected to a new notion of privacy as deficiency. Of course, deficiency, lack, being-deprived, has always been inherent to the concept of the private sphere; in antiquity it was a lack of office, a lack of publicity, a lack of the possibility of political agency. In the sociality of contemporary social media, however, privacy becomes more of a problem because it implies invisibility, the decoupling from the lifeblood of social networks. Felix Stalder describes this new fear of—now digital—disappearance as the reverse side of the promise of authentic communication in social networks:

> In order to create sociability in the space of flows people first
> have to make themselves visible, that is, they have to create their

representation through expressive acts of communication. [...] There are both negative and positive drivers to making oneself visible in such a way: there is the threat of being invisible, ignored and bypassed, on the one hand, and the promise of creating a social network really expressing one's own individuality, on the other.[9]

So rather than supposing the core of the authentic self in privacy and leaving it there, it is sought and produced in the expressive practice of confession in the social networks, in order to also ward off the danger of delivery, disjunction from the life-sustaining social networks. The fully active maintenance of the machinic connection sustains the infrastructure for the manic practice of confession, and at the same time it protects against slipping into the dark fields of activities that are not or are only barely visible and therefore dangerous or simply not commodifiable, because they are not available for valorization.

It is no longer a small number of authority figures that are the addressees of machinic confession, those to whom one confesses in a decidedly personal relationship, but an increasingly larger, often incalculable number of "friends." However, this relationship is only rarely social in the traditional sense—if at all, sociality usually appears in the inverse form of the shitstorm or other abuses on the Internet, as an asocial sociality. Machinic confession persists in the mode of conduct between the self-identifying self and its truth in front of the opaque wall of a social confessional, Facebook. Although Foucault did not know Facebook, he described the way it works very well:

> Its veracity is not guaranteed by the lofty authority of the magistery, nor by the tradition it transmits, but by the bond, the basic intimacy in discourse, between the one who speaks and what he is speaking about. On the other hand, the agency of domination

does not reside in the one who speaks [...], but in the one who listens and says nothing; not in the one who knows and answers, but in the one who [...] is not supposed to know.[10]

The unknowing, incalculable and silent majority of "friends" dominates the scene. Their sharing, as invoked by the Facebook slogan, pledged to be as smooth as possible, "smooth sharing," consists of pressing a button, of clicking on a link, the share button. The effect of the truth discourse, however, is to be found among those who confess something or everything about themselves.

On Nietzsche's scale from compulsion through "voluntary obedience" to "instinct," the movement thus far has gone in the direction of what Nietzsche calls "instinct," which he links, first of all, with habituation, in other words naturalization and normalization, and secondly with pleasure. These two aspects are directly coupled in Facebook's practice: the habituation to machinic appendage concatenates with the machinic desire for total sharing. "Division" functions for Facebook not—or not only—in the sense of the illicit appropriation of personal data by state or economic actors, but also in the desire of the data-producers for dividualization, in a kind of "freely obedient," "voluntary" division, self-determined self-division. Facebook is based on invoking the liberating effect of confession, on the figure of privacy as a deficiency to be avoided and on the presumption that machinic confession is not compelled, but instead implies voluntariness, desire, pleasure, and—with Nietzsche—"vanity."

Multitudes of Data. New Dividual Scales

Nietzsche's view remains, even in the critique of what is all too human, a view of the human being, most of all the individual human being. His thesis of the self-division of man in morality remains stuck—as essentially does also Foucault's ethics of confession—at the question of the compliance of individuals. Yet what social/media technologies like Facebook do cannot be explained solely with a view of human beings or individuals and their relationship to a collective, nor can it be explained with a subjugation of human or non-human individuals to machines. The machinic-dividual itself goes far beyond techno-media apparatuses and individual desires.

Nietzsche wrote: "In morality man treats himself not as individuum but as dividuum." Yet there is no "dividuum." In the strong substantive sense, "the dividuum" does not exist: as in the philological evidence, in which the Latin word occurs only rarely, and even then only as a weak, heteronomous substantive, it makes little sense to speak of "a dividual" or "dividuals." Even "in morality," individuals cannot become dividuals, but in and through dividualization they can indeed become conforming, compliant, obedient individuals. "In morality" ever new forms of subservience, of conformity, of adaptation emerge, ever new "compliant characters," yet this subservience, insofar as it remains at the level of the individual, does not grasp the dividual.

Over a hundred years after Nietzsche, Gilles Deleuze posits the transition from the disciplinary to the control regime with a similar formulation relating to the concept of the dividual. With this he takes up the ideas of his friend Michel Foucault, with whom he was jointly responsible for the critical French edition of Nietzsche's complete works. According to Deleuze's explanations in the "Postscript on the Societies of Control," the disciplinary regime has two poles, in which it is equally interested. It masses together and individualizes, constituting the mass as a body and modularizing its members as individuals—entirely in keeping with Nietzsche's notions of morality and the self-dividing individual, entirely in keeping with Foucault's interpretation of the mode of governing of pastoral power: *omnes et singulatim*. Deleuze reformulates this equal interest of pastoral power in its two poles: the disciplinary society is marked at the individual pole by the signature, as unequivocal indication of the thereby identifiable author, and at the mass pole by the number or administrative numeration [*numéro matricule*] that identifies the position of the individual in the mass. It is this relation, by no means oppositional, but rather mutual, between "single-ones" and "one-all," which is exemplarily attributed to the compositions of German Romanticism in *A Thousand Plateaus*, in which the groupings of power are fully diversified, but only as "relations proper to the universal."[11] The romantic hero acts as a subjectified individual under the conditions of an orchestral whole. Always *omnes*, all as one, one-all, orchestra—*et*, and—*singulatim*, single-ones, single voices, related to the one-all.

A completely different regime is that in which the mass is individuated by group individuations and cannot be reduced to the individuality of the subjects and the universality of the whole—in *A Thousand Plateaus* Deleuze and Guattari describe this completely different relation of (now no longer one-all, but rather) dividual one-crowd and single-one with musical examples from Debussy, Mussorgsky, Bartok, and Berio. Here the mass is not individuated by persons, but by affects, and to this extent the single-one is not individual and related to the universal, but rather singular. Deleuze developed the dark side of this new "dividual scale"[12] a decade after *A Thousand Plateaus* in the "Postscript on the Societies of Control"—and Nietzsche still seems to sound through Deleuze's formulation: "Individuals have become 'dividuals,' and masses [have become] samples, data, markets, or 'banks'."[13]

That which is dividual (unlike Nietzsche, Deleuze uses the adjective dividual) and the banks, though banks are meant to a lesser extent in the traditional sense, and more so as databases: yet not only the bank as a place populated by counters, clerks and payment forms seems oddly outmoded to today's ears, when describing dividual data flows in the societies of control. Even the image of the database still contains far too much of a territorium that can be clearly situated, a storage space that is administered, arranged and ruled by human beings. The reality of today's dividual data sets, enormous accumulations of data that can be divided, recomposed and valorized in endless ways, is one of worldwide streams, of deterritorialization and of machinic expansion, most succinctly expressed as Big Data. Facebook needs the self-division of individual users just as intelligence agencies continue to retain individual identities. Big Data, on the other hand, is less interested in individuals and just as little interested in a totalization of data, but all the more so in data sets that are freely floating and as detailed as possible, which it can dividually traverse—as an open field of immanence with a potentially endless extension. These enormous multitudes of data want to form a horizon of knowledge that governs the entire past and present and so is also able to capture the future.

The collection of data by economic and state actors, especially secret services, insurance and banking industries, has a long tradition, but it has gained a completely new quality with machine-readability and the machinic processing of the data material. This quality applies not only to credit rating agencies or intelligence agencies, but also to all areas of networked everyday life, all partial data of individual lives, about children, divorces, debts, properties, consumption habits, communication behaviors, travelling habits, internet activities, movements in real space, whereabouts, health, fitness, eating habits, calorie consumption, dental care, credit card charges, cash machine use, to name only a few. Refrigerators, ovens, thermostats, smart-guide toothbrushes, intelligent toilet bowls, networked offices, networked kitchens, networked bedrooms, networked bathrooms, networked toilet facilities—all controllable via smartphone, all accessible via cloud. This machinic data can potentially be combined, for instance for the logistics of individual thing-movements, and made accessible according to dividual logics.

In order to traverse, divide and recombine these data, cooperation is needed from those who were previously called consumers. Participation means the most comprehensible free (especially in the sense of unpaid) data exchange possible, not only sharing existing data, but also producing new data. Data valorization plays out in the terrain of externalizing production processes and activating consumers, as it has been intensified since the 1990s in all economic areas. Crowds, multitudes, dispersed masses—their modes of existence and living are captured, stretched, appropriated and exploited beyond the realm of paid labor. Scoring, rating, ranking, profiling. Consumers who are activated and generate value with their activity do not have to be paid. The open source model of program development by the crowd has meanwhile become established as a business model and spread to all economic sectors. Free labor in free association, but to the advantage of the enterprises of the New Economy.

And instead of the added value thereby produced being invested in higher wages, the "free labor" of the freelance data brokers results in exactly the opposite consequences, namely a further devaluing and elimination of paid labor. The economy of partition and domination becomes a no less dominating economy of dividing/sharing, boosted by self-government. A sharing economy that lifts the minus of community from the Christian genealogy into contemporary machinic capitalism. Appeals to cut spending, degrowth compulsion, austerity by other means.

The economy of sharing/dividing data commodifies not only automatically accruing and occurring data, it also stimulates the production of data beyond all professional activity. This has been easy to track recently in the context of physical self-measurement and bookkeeping about body data. In my old-fashioned format of Kieser Training, this bookkeeping is still limited to an analog procedure. The machines appear as relatively plain and at least not visibly networked apparatuses for bodily fitness, which are explained as rationally as possible in both their function and effect and enable concentrated individual training without disruption. But the machine is not only the mechanical equipment in which I harness myself, it is especially the board onto which I clamp in the table where I note my small steps of progress. Whether there is progress or regress raises the tension, the pressure, the desire. In the desire of appending to, being harnessed in the machines, it happens that I overheat. Self-division functions well here, data division not yet.

The concurrence of individuals measuring themselves on the one hand and producing dividual body data on the other remained reserved to the Quantified Self movement. Whereas the confessional techniques of self-government in social media primarily produce discursive outputs, their quantitative representations consisting mostly in the number of likes, the permanent measuring of the self is to be commodified directly and simply as the production of quantitative data. First of all, Quantified Self implies observing oneself as permanently as possible. Together with confessional literature and lifelogging, the machinic connection of physical and discursive self-techniques is probably even more relevant than that of the lineages that link the single techniques with their historical genealogies: the Quantified Self with the old growth marks on the door frame, the charts of weight measurements from the family scale, and other classical body records, lifelogging with writing log books, diaries, travel journals, and other records. Yet a further combination drives the commodification to an extreme: feeding quantitative and qualitative data into the social networks, with the speed of their feedback adding aspects of sociality and social control to the individual privacy of body data and the discursive narratives.

A further zone of the expansion of dividual data is that of search engines. What is searched is perhaps not so interesting in itself, but the accumulation of search data determines both individual and dividual forms of data processing. Machinic search processes lead by principle to the probable, to what is dominant for the majority, to what is normalized and certainly to what is economically lucrative for the search engines. Google & Co. tailor search results individually (geographical position, language, individual search history, personal profile, etc.), but also in keeping with their commercial interests. Over time, all the individual profiles become increasingly valuable as part of Big Data. In theory, however, searching is still determined too much by humans and thus dangerously uncontrolled. This is why there is currently a massive transition to machinic industries of recommendation, which save the consumers the trouble of engaging in a relatively undetermined search process. Before users even begin to think of searching, they can count on recommendations. These recommendations are not always presented to the customers by fully automatized systems: algorithms often collaborate with humans to develop fine gradations and endless combinations of possibilities based on the previous habits not only of the individual customers, but also of their social and territorial surroundings. The results are unrequested and yet suitable individualized recommendations for books and other purchases from Amazon, travel recommendations from Air Berlin, film recommendations from Netflix, and even these specializations are increasingly dissolving.

The compliant character is receptive to machinic recommendations. Machinic control is expanding as far as it can: everything is suggested, wherever possible there are no more open, unmeasured search movements. Yet not even the boundary between the measurable and the immeasurable is stable. The measuring gauges seek to reach further and further into the immeasurable. Not only the measurable is to be measured, but also as much of the immeasurable as possible is to be shifted into the domain of the measurable. That is the endless desire of the modulating mode of collecting data: to maintain control not only over the measured and measurable territories, but also to penetrate into uncontrolled realms not previously desired and to measure them as exactly and comprehensively as possible. White spots in real and virtual spaces, videos that have not interested anyone before, internet links that have never been clicked on.

The government of the number, the measuring gauge, the standard measure reaches its limitations, and in the regime of control the code therefore replaces the polar system of signature and number: whereas disciplinary regimes are distinguished, according to Deleuze, by the identification and counting of individual bodies and mass-bodies, the signature of the control society is the "coded 'dividual' matter to be controlled."[14] In a story by Guattari, where Deleuze does not interpret the plot as fiction, a city is imagined in which the dystopia of the gated community appears to have been overcome. The city is not divided by barriers, walls, blockades into licit and illicit zones, but is modulated by a machine that records the position of the single elements in an open milieu. Thanks to their dividual electronic cards, those who inhabit the city can leave their apartment, street, neighborhood, but—and this is the catch: "the card may also be rejected on a particular day, or between certain times of day."[15] This is not something like a technical defect, the fragility of the electronic material. There are certain hours or even only seconds, during which certain territories may be entered. That the card is invalid may be due to the individual carrying the card, whose signature does not allow certain movements. Yet perhaps the problem of validity is not even due to the identity and number of the individual, but rather to conspicuous movements of single things and multitudes, which cause the temporary closure of a territory. In this respect, the card itself is less dividual than is the machinic assemblage, the codes of which control the openings and closings of relays, and which move through a large number of individual cards as "dividual matter to be controlled."

[: Ritornello 7: Undulism :]

[: Somewhere in Leningrad, September 2014, a drunken late-summer night. Too late to get a ride with any car. Someone calls a taxi. The taxi driver speaks English. Instead of a taximeter, a complex digital display, indexes, graphics. Dancing bars, wave-like movements, display of dividual lines. He explains that he only drives a taxi on the side, accelerates to 90 km/h and winds his way, skidding a bit, through the hold-ups of the late traffic. He is primarily concerned with trading and algo-trading. The fluctuations on the display are constantly moving, and he seems to be somehow manipulating them. The fog of a twenty milliliters alcohol level blurs with the waves of the stock prices. Faster and faster, I have to throw up. Crash, rip, write-off.

The wave-like [*ondulatoire*], the continuous modulating, the constant deforming of the "human of control" repeats a rare term from Karl Rosenkranz' catalogue of ugliness. In *The Aesthetics of Ugliness* it appears at the beginning of Rosenkranz' discussion of types of formlessness, amorphy, aesthetic shapelessness, the absence of every boundary to the outside. Rosenkranz distinguishes between two different types to conceptualize *becoming as passing*, the shading of the distinction into nothing: whereas in nature the unbounded up and down of the waves can be considered beautiful, in art the *undulistic*, wave-like is an exclusively negative symbol of nebulization, effeminacy, debility.

The undulistic is *the lassitude of delimiting, where it would be decidedly necessary; the opaqueness of the distinction where it should come clearly to the fore; the unintelligible of the expression, where it should be marked.* For Rosenkranz there seems to be a clear line of separation between the natural beauty of transience and an ugly becoming of formlessness, which he states with the terms nebulism and undulism: he charges what is nebulous and insufficiently wave-like with being washed out, fading, and unsettling. In Goethe's essay "The Collector and His Friends" from 1798 the term undulism already appeared as an indication of what is soft, weak, bending. Undulists are like those who do not want to become adults, who play in the waves, artists as well as collectors, lacking earnestness: *They were also called* Serpentine. *This serpentine and soft style manifests itself in artists as well as amateurs by a certain weakness, sleepiness, and if you will, sickly gracefulness. Such works are in demand by those who wish to find in a work of art something that is a little more than nothing at all, who never see the varied colors of a soap bubble in the air without delight. They are wanting in meaning and power, and are therefore generally acceptable, as nullity in society.*

In the age of the mole, modulation was called undulism. The snake was the animal of the societies of control, and the flowing surface of the wave in the water, on land and in air was an excellent medium for wave-riding, skating, sky-surfing. The streams of the algo-trading accelerate, hesitate, go to hell … and recompose themselves again, disintegrating, picking up speed. :]

Algorithm, Logistics, Line

The algorithm sparks capital's old fantasies of ending its dependency on living labor at last. If no longer managers, bankers, brokers, but rather programs carry out calculations and computations and react to these kinds of calculations and computations, then it appears that humans no longer operate with programs, but rather programs with humans. It is not only that they subordinate themselves to machines, that they become part of the machine like the workers in Marx's Fragment on Machines, but that they are to be wholly swept away by the self-expanding fantasy of their screens. This is the image Stefano Harney draws in his text "Algorithmic Institutions and Logistical Capitalism"[16] of the inventive and simultaneously (suicidally) murderous effect of the algorithm. In the fantasy of logistics, things speak directly with things. Reduction of all machinic relations to thing-relationships, inversion of anthropocentrism: instead of human beings, things are essentialized.

Yet Harney also describes how, with the help of the algorithm, long before its expansion in finance, in the operations management of bodies, machines, instruments, trucks, warehouses and factories, our own hands, our own labor, our own desire allowed a world to emerge that wanted to become a world without us. Operations management is the science and practice of the relationship between variable and constant capital *in motion*, perhaps even more influential and insidious in daily life than finance. The assembly line is the starting point for all the considerations of this once marginal area of management theory. And it is the assembly line from which Harney also develops his central concept of the *line*. Workers and machines appear along "the line" by "making" the line. In this way, a more complex puzzle is composed than the perspective on machines, on workers, or even the one-sided relation of the human to the machine. What counts is the machinic relation of humans, machines, and all the other components to the line and its motion. All these components draw the line and are drawn by it, taken into service for the continuous handling and improvement of the process, not for the sake of a static product, but for the incessant optimization of the line.

Logistics is a sub-discipline of operations management, which moves objects, moves itself with objects, moves all the way through objects. The contemporary history of logistics begins with containerization, with the expanded value chain of global markets.

> Logistics, reverse logistics, user communities, and later relationship marketing, came to be seen as part of a continuous process that could be continuously improved before inputs entered the factory, while they were transformed in the factory, and after outputs left the factory.[17]

Concentration on the product, its efficiency and quality, is replaced by a line running in spirals and feedback loops, and its previous linearity and directedness must be rethought: now as an endless, a-linear line, a line going in all directions, a line that collects, accumulates, assembles, no longer an assembly line but a line of assembly.

Working on/in/along the line has multiple implications. Working on the line means, first of all, a certain danger, a constant balancing act. However, there is also an allusion to the digital networking of online work. And when the fantasy of logistics increasingly regards humans as a factor to be eliminated, this does not mean that machinic capitalism functions without humans. For the human components, "the line" implies the expanded assembly line, the *fabbrica sociale*, as it has been formulated in postoperaist theory, the "social factory," which has simultaneously installed itself as the binding bond of a cooperation that has become servile. Christian Marazzi describes this development in its final stage as the all-encompassing implementation of the Google model. This pseudo-horizontal model, which centers no longer on the product, but rather on the relationships between product and consumption, is even expanding into the non-virtual fields of industry and services. It relies—as described above—on the activation of consumers as users, even "in the hyper-material world of the automobile."[18]

Within the enterprise, the line also relates to a vertical line, primarily in the term of line managers. As Harney writes, the main function of the line managers of "algorithmic institutions" consists of operating the algorithmic metrics in a servile manner. Even if the word strategy comes up in all corners of the enterprise, it has been completely hollowed out in its meaning of managers acting strategically. Instead of proceeding strategically, as in the past, the task of management now consists of minimizing exposure to the error-proneness and slowness of human decisions. Managers literally do not know what they are doing. They try to keep the line in motion, in the end merely to execute it so as not to disrupt the algorithmic institution:

> Typically such an institution has deployed algorithmic metrics to the point where line managers are entirely deskilled and can act only as enforcers and police within the institutions. They set no direction, and have no explanation for the direction the

organisation takes. They are consequently and typically defensive, bullying, insecure, and reduced to mouthing phrases from the institution's leader. They appear to be micro-managing but in fact this is only the metrics possessing them and operating through them.[19]

The incomprehension of everything that is to be conveyed from top to bottom goes with vertical servility, deskilling with policing postures. Meanwhile, at least in the fantasy of operations management and company leaders, the algorithms exercise self-management, successors to the Marxian automatic subject. Only one task remains for management, both old and new: line managers are mostly concerned with protecting the algorithmic self-organization from the resistance of the workers. The compliant character is pre-destined to keep the entire assemblage compliant.

And finally, working on the line also literally means working on the line itself, constantly improving and expanding it, appending something to it, all the way to the point of "setting a new line." That is also the new function of the leading management, the bosses, who are not managers but leaders. Due to its complexity they can no longer command the enterprise. Setting a line now means interpreting the line, narrating it like a story. Following the line, understanding it in following and narrating it in understanding, they trace it, redraw it with each new turn, with each sudden break, with each unexpected leap. In this paradoxical logic, leading means following the line. The constant reforming and deforming of the line is the omnipresent foundation for working on it. If the line is continuously improved in every moment of the present, then its future is also to be determined. Metrics replaces measurement, the algorithm relies on a new relative, derived, derivative, metrical measurement that measures efficiency only to speculate with it.

The ongoing modulation and smoothing of the measurement, the incessant recalculation needs the complex logic of the algorithm. In this way, the line becomes a speculative line: not one that primarily has the value of a commodity, a business, a corporation in view, but rather the process and the speculation with the line itself. What the line becomes is the goal of all computations.

Lastly, the line is also the abstract-dividual line that traverses many single things. It connects not only the social factory as a new assembly line, it also collects, combines the parts of diverse single things that fit together to derive added value from this new arrangement. In his book *Knowledge LTD*, Randy Martin writes about this inversion of the classical production process:

> The mass assembly line gathered all its inputs in one place to build a tightly integrated commodity that was more than the sum of its parts. Financial engineering played this process in reverse, disassembling a commodity into its constituent and variable elements and dispersing these attributes to be bundled together with the elements of other commodities of interest to a globally oriented market for risk-managed exchange. Each of these movable parts is reassembled by risk attribute so that they become worth more as derivatives than their individual commodities [...].[20]

Logistics is no longer content with economic diagrams and flows, with calculations and predictions, with representations that precede the action of the managers. As Stefano Harney and Fred Moten write in *Undercommons*, it not only wants to purify the flow of goods from human time and human error, but to live in the concrete itself, in space at once, in time at once, in form at once.[21] In this run on the concrete, mathematical calculations no longer simply calculate risks to control and minimize them, but instead play with ever greater risks. They are supposed to see into the future, produce futures, calculate probabilities based on currently achievable data. What is improbable can nevertheless occur, and then it is called a "black swan."[22] In this respect, improbability is still within the framework of managing and exploiting risks, which now no longer apply solely to the subsistential risk of vulnerability, of precariousness, but also to derivatives or secondary risks that can arise in the collection and recombination of large masses of data, machinic-dividual risks.

At the same time, the algorithms are always on the prowl for what lies outside their territory and its im/probabilities, veritably defined by what they are not yet and what they may possibly never become. And the traders of the *Blank Swan*[23] are hounding along with them when they create, under/write, draw up derivative contracts virtually out of nothing: whereas black and white swans are based on probabilities, the blank swan is the animal of the unknowable, what is outside the realm of every probability calculation. For the ex-trader Elie Ayache, the blank swan is the non-knowledge of the future, which has become the market. The human factor of machinic capitalism, in this perspective, consists in creating the event of drawing/writing: the work of the traders consists in writing and drawing the derivative as a *creatio ex nihilo*. The image of the preconditionless *tabula rasa* permeates their fantasies. Without prior knowledge, foresight or predictions, they transport themselves, according to Ayache, into the future.

And the relationship to the future still stands at the center. Even though it is supposed to be a future without predictions, the traders in hot pursuit of the future forget about the present. Just like the white swan and the black swan, the blank swan remains in the logic of algorithmics and logistics, always on the prowl for what it is not. "There is some/thing logistics is always after," write Harney and Moten, and in a slight shifting motion that is typical for them, they call this before, this outside of, this beyond of logistics—deviating only a little from its harried opponent, eternally algorithmically catching up: logisticality.[24]

Derivatives. Subprime Crisis, Debt Crisis, Financial Crisis

In the mode of patriarchal partition and of *dividuom facere*, as well as in the pastoral panorama of disciplinary power, minted money and gold rule as the standard measure. The control regime, on the other hand, refers, according to Deleuze, to floating rates of exchange, to modulations that introduce a percentage of diverse standard currencies as codes. Today betting on exchange rates, on whether they rise or fall, implies an endless mode of dismembering and recomposing the dividual line.

The US subprime crisis of 2006 and 2007 has often been interpreted in a one-sidedly moralistic way, at least in Europe. Here the simple irresponsibility of bankers who did not check their customers closely enough, there the stupid, enticed, seduced debtors who borrowed money they would never have. Much is wrong with this image, including the general assumption of the stupidity of those affected, the false assessment of the banking business as morally conditioned, the misperception of the development of financial instruments, which occurred not only in the crisis years in a narrower sense, but at least over the last two decades. Most of all, however, the premise that the banks assumed extreme risks *en masse* without questioning or being questioned cannot be upheld after taking a closer look at the machinic operations of financialization. The group of stereotypes around the predations of "predatory capitalism" and the platitude of "predatory lending" as well as the stubborn insistence on a separation between real economy and financial economy both belong to this problem complex of the false, because purely moral, interpretation of the course of events. In contrast, with Angela Mitropoulos and her radical re-interpretation of the financial crisis as "usury from below" in *Contact and Contagion*, a decided subject status can indeed be attributed to those "affected" by the subprime-crisis: "It is too easy to assume that those who took out the loans had no sense of risk or, rather, did not strategise within the cramped conditions of what was a monetised, racialised and gendered housing regime well before the advent of subprime loans." The disorganized power of the subprime class could conversely be described as effective: "The subprime class rolled over their debts and lived beyond their means, generating surplus in the most unproductive of ways."[25]

In a longer essay on "The Wealth of Dividuals in the Age of the Derivative," Arjun Appadurai discusses, among other things, aspects of dividualization that relate to financial politics.[26] He locates both the "rise of the dividual" and the "erosion of the individual" in the early 1970s, when the term "dividual" also appeared in anthropological literature. Especially the effects of the spread of the derivative as a central tool of finance capitalism since the 1990s produced, according to Appadurai, a predative form of dividualism ("predative dividualism" in contrast to "progressive dividualism" or "truly socialized dividualism"), which in the multiplication of its more opaque and completely unreadable processes evades every check, every regulation, every social or democratic control. As Appadurai explains the complex course of the subprime crisis:

> Even a simple housing mortgage is a mysterious thing. It is an instrument of home 'ownership' in which the so-called home-owner owns only the mortgage but not the house, except at the end point of a long horizon of amortization, which is itself a somewhat mysterious mechanism. Meanwhile the lending bank is

the real owner [...]. Meanwhile the cost of this peculiar form of co-ownership is borne by the mortgage owner in the form of interest, which is substantially the profit of the bank. [...] The bizarre materiality of the mortgage-backed American house is that while its visible material form is relatively fixed, bounded and indivisible, its financial form, the mortgage, has now been structured to be endlessly divisible, recombinable, saleable and leverage-able for financial speculators, in a manner that is both mysterious and toxic.[27]

This highly abstract, dividual aspect of housing was abstracted to a further stage through the introduction of a new, central mechanism: the derivative is a financial instrument that is "derived" from the price of other commodities, which by principle speculates with the possible, future value of a commodity. With the complication of the derivative as an endlessly continuing series of derivatives of derivatives, the instrument became a machinic tool of trading with risks, of betting on risks. In this way, housing mortgages were also drawn into a huge wave of derivatives, the values of which were completely disproportionate to the real values of the homes.

Most of all, the introduction of specific derivatives, which allowed many first-time homeowners to get mortgages, was the reason for this gigantic gulf between the value of a home and a derivative. The subprime crisis got its name from the fact that many banks gave mortgages to people whose credit rating was "subprime." In her text on "The Subprime Crisis and the Gender-Specific Debt Trap," Brigitte Young describes the very gendered and racialized conditions for subprime loans, which contradict the context of their genesis in the anti-discrimination laws of the 1970s. Access to cheaper real estate loans for all strata of society was fought for as a "civil right to property" over a period of decades, but these politics envisioned as egalitarian and emancipatory also cleared the way for the gendered and racialized mechanisms that led to the crisis and the "debt trap."

> What is tragic is that at the very moment when women and minorities became integrated into the financial value appreciation of the real estate market through massive private debt, it then was increasingly the lower-income groups, following the motto "last in, first out," who lost their highly mortgaged real estate to fore-closure sales.[28]

The granting of mortgages to lower-income groups can therefore be explained on the one hand from a longer genealogy of struggles for equality in relation to a right to housing, and on the other from the fact that after 1990 the finance industries assessed at increasingly high values the potential of the housing market in the brokering of new derivative instruments. Arjun Appadurai describes how mortgage-backed and asset-backed securities made it possible to bundle greater numbers of mortgages, how their assessment became increasingly complex and their masses were also used to "launder" subprime mortgages as they were mixed with other mortgages and thus hidden. At the same time, the instrument of collateralized default obligation "allowed these bundles of mortgages to be divided into tranches or levels which had different credit ratings. What is important, though technically a shade more obscure, is how the higher value tranches were used to bury, obscure or disguise the more toxic tranches."[29] The entire architecture of derivatives made it possible to enormously expand the overall credit volumes of the credit institutes through these practices of obfuscation.

Whereas single things can stay in their place or move, the traffic of derivatives goes in all directions. This is a hypercomplex process of bundling and dividing, which is steered by equally complex combinations of technical and social machines. In comparison with the process of industrial production, one could say that, here too, various specialized procedures produce new investment goods by assembling, mounting, composing parts.[30] Yet in the financial-economic logic of derivatives there is also the reverse process: along with the composition, the process of disassembling is just as important as the complete openness and unpredictability of the product.

For the entire multi-stage process of deriving, dismembering and recomposing, Appadurai uses the metaphor of a house with a beautiful view from the top floor, but with a leaky basement. What is interesting about his depiction is the fact that this leak is produced by an instrument that disassembles many houses, rearranges their parts, and disguises all the leaky basements with the beautifying depiction of a few top floors. That is exactly the logic of dividuality as traversing dividual parts (in multiple aggregate states, here liquid and firm), instead of connecting individual wholes. The underwater mortgages became a disaster for many mortgage owners in 2006 and 2007, and as if this were not enough, the derivative as a financial instrument affected not only the domain of housing, but also nutrition, health, education, the environment and much more. The collapse of the entire US financial system could only be prevented in the first weeks of the Obama administration by huge sums of public money, which led to the debt crisis of European states, especially Greece.

In the standard interpretation of the financial crisis, the derivative is simply one technical aspect of the financial business among many, controlled by the machineoid efficiency of the market and the rational information processing of mathematical programs: only the flight of the derivative from this, its rightful place, so it is said in the standard interpretation, turned it into the instrument of a few greedy persons, into a self-replicating magical broom which the sorcerer's apprentices, the regulators, had left unattended for a moment, allowing it to lose control. But similarly to how it would be wrong to consider finance as separate from the "real world" or the "real economy," to which one would have to return in order to reestablish the moral integrity of the economy, the idea of a machine of derivatives taking on a life of its own is a sub-complex representation.

Today the finance economy is on a par with the production of goods and services and permeates all economic procedures. The automobile industry, for instance, today depends less on the technical optimization of production processes than it does, on the one hand, on relationships to users based on activation and affects, and on the corporations' own in-house financing businesses, on the other.[31] Of course derivatives cannot be eaten or lived in, but the roundly longed-for return to real economy, re-industrialization, re-materialization is certainly not an escape route that is open as a solution to the multiple crises of the present. Disentangling real economy and finance economy has become just as impossible as the Marxist separation between industrial and ficititious profits or that between a productive and an immaterial sector. Marazzi's thesis focuses instead on financialization as one side of the more general modulation described here as machinic capitalism:

> Financialization is not an unproductive and/or parasitic detour to growing shares in added value and collective reserves, but rather the form of the accumulation of capital that corresponds to the new processes of production and value creation.[32]

Arjun Appadurai interprets the success story of the derivatives as the invention of not only a new instrument of finance, but also a new form of mediation. The derivative mediates the distance between commodity and asset, which consists in the not-yet-realized potential of the commodity for future profit.

> Mediated in the capitalist market, the house becomes the mortgage; further mediated, the mortgage becomes an asset, itself subject to trading as an uncertainly priced future commodity. Mediated yet again, this asset becomes part of an asset-backed security, a new derivative form, which can be further exchanged in its incarnation as a debt-obligation.[33]

Appadurai's interpretation is in many respects extremely insightful, but on some aspects I think it would be good to push it beyond itself. The terminology of "predatory dividualism" is too strongly marked by the phantasy of a linear development from a pre- and extra-capitalist, non-western dividuality to a tamed capitalism of the welfare state, further to a post-industrial predatory capitalism and finally to its vaguely suggested transformation into a "progressive dividualism." Most of all, however, Appadurai emphasizes various forms of quantification, especially in the form of monetization, as the central mode of operation in "predatory dividualism."

It is certainly the case that contemporary finance makes use of dividual forms that are produced through quantification. And yet this emphasis on quantification is not without a certain nostalgia for the person as a whole and an implicit sympathy for the sovereign individual of capitalistic modernism that only now, in the dividual crisis, is in danger of becoming just a number. But the focus on quantification considers only one side of a more general process of modulation: the modularization of all processes as counting, measuring, striating. What eludes this perspective is the other side of modulation, the constant modulating that is not only to be understood as an ancillary operation for obscuring quantification, but which results in an independent, though complementary effect: it smoothes all possible reterritorialization attempts, also those of the self-determined streaking of time and space.

What Appadurai calls mediation is not a procedure of introducing a mediating third between the differences, not the insertion and fusion of something in the middle as in *Timaeus*, but rather a procedure of adjusting, aligning, unifying difference, a procedure of modulation. The mode of modulation is both: a striating, standardizing, modularizing procedure, but at the same time also permanently reforming, modulating right through the forms and striations, a constant movement of re-formation and de-formation. Modularization is striating reterritorialization and social subjugation, a clean separation and disciplining of times and spaces, the production of ever more detailed modules, the implementation of standard measures. Modulating, on the other hand, is servile deterritorialization and machinic subservience, an inseparable, endless, unbounded modulating, an invocation to varying and smoothing the self.

Even if modularizing and modulating seem to be described as completely opposite procedures, they interlock as double modulation. Striating time and space in all directions in ever more detail, measuring smaller and smaller parts, endlessly reducing the scales, conforms with breaching measure all the way to the immeasurable valorization and smoothing of time and space. Stratifying, striating and counting all relationships, bringing every single module into form, at the same time gliding from one key into another, translating into as yet unknown languages, interlocking all possible levels.

And this is also the crossroad where the tipping point of similarity becomes relevant again as a crucial precondition for measurability. Modulating, qualitative adaptation is a possibility condition of quantifying, measuring, modularizing. Introducing measure is only possible through similarity processes of assimilation and comparison, processes of *Eineln* [unifying].[34] Similarity as approximation and assimilation is the modulating process that is necessary to establish new modes of counting, striating and modularizing in the first place. Qualitative assimilation as precondition for quantitative gradation.

At the same time, modulating assimilation does not function through the similarity of individuals. It is thus not a one-sided matter of what cultural pessimists often call leveling. There are levels that are simultaneously larger and smaller, more and less than the individual, the abstract lines traversing single things, machinically scanning them and rearranging the parts according to their similarities: dividual lines, dividual machines. When similarity tips, modulates into the measurable, then from a possible nexus of social intercourse it can also become a principle of order. And if it has become that, then it is recognized—as Foucault writes with a view to Descartes and Deleuze—by *bon sens*, because this is "the world's most effective agent" of partition: it "recognizes the similar, the exactly similar and the least similar, the greatest and the smallest, the brightest and the darkest,"[35] and its recognition is identification, conversion of similarity into identity, transformation of the potentially different into the potentially same. A new "age of comparison" dawns, but completely different from Nietzsche's depiction of it as people's "outward restlessness, their mingling together with one another, the polyphony of their endeavors" (*All Too Human*, I.1.23): much more it is an age that presses polyphony into a comparable tonality, seeking to turn the consonance of the similar into unison harmony.

The derivative is here more than a contract about the exchange of a certain amount of commodities at a certain future point in time and at a certain price. It is the instrument that, counter to the notion of a separation between financial markets and real economy, establishes the connection of all disparate economic sectors and types of capital, makes them commensurable with one another and subjects them to a common measure. As Randy Martin writes:

> Yet if commodities appeared as a unit of wealth that could abstract parts into a whole, derivatives are a still more complex process by which parts are no longer unitary, but are continuously disassembled and reassembled as various attributes are bundled and their notional value exceeds the whole economy to which they may once have been summed. Shifts in scale from concrete to abstract or local to global are no longer external yardsticks of equivalence. They are internal to the circulation of the bundled attributes that derivative transactions multiply and set in motion.[36]

Dividualization of economy in every magnitude. Commensurability and comparability must be established in order to valorize the dividual exchange.

Queer Debts: Spread, Usury, Excess

"[...] a new habit [...] is gradually implanting itself in us on the same soil and will in thousands of years' time perhaps be strong enough to bestow on mankind the power of bringing forth the wise, guiltless (conscious of innocence) man as regularly as it now brings forth—*not his antithesis but necessary preliminary*—the unwise, unjust, guilt-conscious man." (Nietzsche, *All Too Human*, 1.2.107)

Whereas the individual component recedes into the background in machinic capitalism, the patriarchal logic of partition is by no means suspended under dividual conditions. As was clearly recognizable in the subprime crisis, racialized, gendered, national and geopolitically conditioned forms of separation have become increasingly effective means for achieving hierarchical differentiation, social cleavages and radical marginalization. An extreme one-sidedness is evident in the conditions with respect to both lending practices and the foreclosures and waves of evictions since 2007 from homes whose mortgages could not be repaid. For Christian Marazzi, the potential participation of entire populations, including those who can provide no securities, is a necessary precondition to the derivative system comparable with "a sort of Ponzi scheme or an air-plane game in which those who came in last allow those who came in first to be remunerated."[37] The better asset values of the wealthy were supported by the growing debts of the impoverished, so that mathematical risk models ultimately determined who had a roof over their head.

The derivative system and the financial and debt crises largely resulting from it have reinforced and accelerated the unequal distribution of wealth and made the world of machinic capitalism an even more insecure place for many. Driving the primacy of stock prices and dividends to the extreme, the hyperproductivist logic of financialization impels the colonization of the present. Derivatives engender a condition of exacerbated risk, of debt, of dependencies through and beyond different times and spaces. To subsistential division have been added the dividual effects of financialization, bets on risks, derivative machinations in machinic capitalism.

All of this calls for a reappropriation of the present that carries us to the other side of dividual economy. How, then, can economy be envisioned as not based on individual property, on the dis/possession of each and every individual, but as using the abstract-dividual line to compose new forms of sociality? An economy that implies forms of distribution other than dividends as claims of shareholders: a dividend beyond the realm of measures and metrics, of modularizing and modulating, of number and code, where that which is to be distributed is not well ordered by "common sense," as the "best distribution," but rather as an ever broader and wilder distribution, spread, dispersion, logisticality, proliferation of social wealth? What if Deleuze and Foucault were wrong, if similarity could be tipped again, if it were not eternally marked as betrayer of the measureless difference and as transition to measurability, but rather as the potential of a resistive form of dividuality?

In 1933, the year the National Socialists took power in Germany, Walter Benjamin wrote a short essay of not much more than five pages entitled "Doctrine of the Similar." While the title might suggest a more extensive treatise, in its intensity and conceptual richness the text is by no means disappointing. Benjamin does not mention the political time to which the text refers, but does point to a "powerful compulsion to become similar and also to behave mimetically." In terms of developmental psychology this applies to the child that increasingly conforms to its territorial surroundings, in terms of cultural history to the compulsion to adapt in delimited communities, in terms of contemporary history to the fascist aesthetics of an instrumental and leveling similarity, which serves as transition to uniformity and totalizing enclosure. Yet despite this evidence of similarity compelling conformism, Benjamin does not reject the term, and instead contrasts the compulsion to adaptation, assimilation, compliance, which are supposed to be produced by means of similarity, with a concept of non-pliable similarity. He calls this similarity a "non-sensuous similarity" and attributes to it the ability to create "tensions" [*Verspannungen*].

In order to invent the other side of the dividual economy, this tipping of similarity from the compulsion to comply into something non-pliable is tremendously significant. There are different responses and first conceptual proposals for developing struggles over this form of similarity, over a similarity that does not serve to hand over the non-measurable to the quantitative order of equivalence. What all these proposals have in common is that they venture into a vague terrain and cannot and will not anticipate the practices of a dividual economy.

In *The Violence of Financial Capitalism*, Christian Marazzi points out the productive contradictions between the rights of social property and the rights of private property. The formula 2+28 that is conventional in lending contracts, for instance, means that the mortgage interest in the first two years mirrors the use value, only to be dominated for the next twenty-eight years by the exchange value. The practice of the first two years is an indicator of the right to housing, which is all the more brutally negated in the years that follow.

In such a way, the financial logic produces a common (goods) that it then divides and privatizes through the expulsion of the 'inhabitants of the common' by means of the artificial creation of scarcity of all kinds—scarcity of financial means, liquidity, rights, desire, and power.[38]

New forms of resistance and instituent practices have crystallized against these violent consequences, such as Strike Debt in the US or the protests against evictions and occupations of buildings by the Plataforma de Afectados por la Hipoteca (PAH) in Spain.[39] Especially the right to housing and the debts of those who claim this right have resulted not only in collective resistance and aid against evictions, but also in molecular everyday practices that reverse the concept of debt. This reversal takes on various conceptual forms, in Marazzi's approach the form of "social rent":

> In other words, if up until today, the access to a common good had taken the form of *private debt*, from now on it is legitimate to conceive (and reclaim it) the same right in the form of *social rent*. In financial capitalism, social rent assumes the form of redistribution, the way in which society gives everyone the right to live with dignity. As such, social rent is articulable on many terrains, particularly on that of education and access to knowledge in the form of the right to a *guaranteed education income*.[40]

Behind these demands for social rent and a reversal of debt there is also an idea of subsistential division, in which a specific form of mutual indebtedness becomes ineluctable. Debt is certainly the first means for harnessing people into the machines, for the plying of compliant characters, the earlier, the more effectively. At the same time, however, debt is also a terrain of molecular revolution.[41]

Stefano Harney and Fred Moten understand debt in this sense as a component of mutuality and sociality, counter to the asocial loan, which is the means of privatization:

> It is not credit we seek nor even debt but bad debt which is to say real debt, the debt that cannot be repaid, the debt at a distance, the debt without creditor, the black debt, the queer debt, the criminal debt. Excessive debt, incalculable debt, debt for no reason, debt broken from credit, debt as its own principle.[42]

Although it may seem difficult to arrive at a paradoxically positive concept of "bad" or "queer" debt, it goes beyond the concept of social rent, which still remains—however pertinent—a demand made to the state, a demand for redistribution mediated by the state. The concept of queer debt is based on mutual indebtedness (without making use of the moral concept of debt as guilt), and at the same time it means an offensive practice of making debts, of debt excess without consideration of profits.

"Unpaid debt, very simply put, holds out the possibility of 'living beyond one's means' when the means of re-/production are no longer in one's easy reach,"[43] writes Angela Mitropoulos about the spread of debt as a potential crisis of capitalist futurity. She analyzes the surprising reappearance of the term usury in the moral discourses of the crisis since 2007 as an index of debts that are denounced as being immoderate, exorbitant and illegitimate, because their repayment is not guaranteed. Whereas potentially redeemable debt attempts to make the future a calculable version of the present, the return of the medieval sin of usury implies an incalculable, unknowable and possibly inflationary risk.[44] In her study Mitropoulos links this usury of risk with practices and narratives of contagion in the world of finance. Whereas the connectedness of financial institutions used to be considered a mutual insurance against liquidity shocks, after the financial crises of 1997 in parts of Asia and the multiple crises since 2007, it is now conversely regarded as an epidemic danger of toxic assets and subjective risks. In narratives of "counter-" or "unnatural generation," the "absence of productivity," and the "magical accumulation of money," there is a resonance of the disruptive danger of immorality breaking into economy. Dangerous epidemics of queer debts shine even through the nervous, exaggerated and partly anti-Semitic return of the moral discourse on usury. Indeed, talk of usury is also concerned with viral sociality and contagious spreading, in short the proliferation of a "usury from below": "Usury lives in the pores of production because that is where many live, or attempt to."[45]

Mitropoulous, too, emphasizes the significance of debts being subsistential : "[…] it is for the most part the debt that might be understood in terms of the irreducible, incalculable inter-dependence of sharing a world."[46] This potentiality of mutual indebtedness, contagion and dispersion in space and time is what Randy Martin seeks not only in the transformation of debts into social rent, queer debts or usury, but also at the very center of financialization, directly as a social potential of derivatives. If derivatives bundle parts that subsist broadly dispersed from one another, then this first raises the question of why and how this specific feature of derivatives can be transferred to fields other than economics, why and to what end the incalculable, the derivative, can be conceptualized as the basis for social wealth. Martin formulates his answer in three parts: first, for conceptualizing the fragmented, dispersed, isolated as mutually connected without appearing as a unified whole—this is the burning question of the concatenation of singularities in dispersed production, with Marx's traditional image of small-holding peasants as potatoes: of a political recomposition of dispersed potatoes that now do not even end up next to one another in a sack of potatoes; second, to articulate the value of our labor in the midst of transience, instability and volatility—at this point Martin condenses the technical composition of production as being radically in motion; third, to recognize the agency of arbitrage, the small interventions in developing, in writing the derivatives, interventions that are small but nevertheless make a significant difference, entering into a "generative risk" against the backdrop of a "generalized failure."[47]

The interior of the traditional field of economics, according to Martin, was never to be understood as the terrain of the spread and dominance of derivatives. On the contrary, Martin attempts to describe derivatives as exterior to economy, which led to the crisis of economy and economics, to a recession of their empire, with derivatives even as their gravediggers. If derivatives execute the dispossession of the self and of property, then good old possessive individualism is also put in its grave. With the crises of the last decade, the economy is increasingly coming undone, and derivatives are both the catalyst and object of this disintegration: "Derivatives issue from that breach, rendering the political inseparable from wealth creation, and disintegrating the givenness of national populations while opening other prospects for mutual association."[48] Rather than as in the traditional view, which sees derivatives as a phantasmal break of linear time and colonization of the future, these are instead lateral movements and new concatenations of spaces. The derivative sociality appears as transnational in the strong sense—beyond nationality, as a prospect of a completely different form of concatenation at the planetary level. "While derivatives are devised in a language of *futures* and forwards, of anticipating what is to come in the present [...], the act of bundling attributes together speaks of a lateral orientation, which is an effect of intercommensurability."[49] The abstract line of the derivative is drawn toward all sides, as a deterritorialization of the border, as a machinic-dividual concatenation of parts that do not seem to belong together. The temporality of the social logic of the derivative is less the anticipation of the future in futures than it is an expanded present that spreads out in multilateral and mutual exchange in the here and now.

It is not necessary to fully embrace Randy Martin's hopeful interpretations in order to understand derivatives perhaps less as a promise of salvation than as symptoms of a change that engenders new openings—without any assurance as to whether these openings might flow into wholly new forms of dominating partition and participation, or into modes of existence in which Martin rightly recognizes the social logic of the derivatives as "an excess that is released but never fully absorbed, noise that need not be stilled, a debt registered yet impossible to repay."[50] If the many steal away from the pressures of credit, draw lines of flight in and out of the field of immanence of machinic capitalism, if queer and bad debts proliferate—why shouldn't the very dividuality of derivatives demonstrate that even in the mode of modulation, forms of subjectivation emerge that elude assimilation, conformism and compliance?

IV. CONDIVISION

Traversing the Times.
The De/Anthropologization of Dividuality

Human beings comprising multiple individuals, individuals comprising multiple human beings, dividual lines crossing countless human beings and single things, dividual lines traversing time and connecting human beings with their ancestors. It was only a question of time that the dividual became established in the theory of human beings: since the 1970s sporadic and geographically dispersed studies have been published in the field of anthropology on the diachronous or synchronous division of the person. Criticizing reductive terms of the idiosyncratic individual, sometimes explicitly problematizing possessive individualism as an occidentalist-capitalist construction, most of these positions seek alternative conceptualizations of personhood in their ethnological field research.

In 1971 the South African social anthropologist Meyer Fortes published an essay on the concept of the person as an aspect of his many years of ethnographic research among the Tallensi of West Africa.[1] He insists on a Maussian notion of the person as more a "microcosm of social order" than a holistically integrated individual. This notion allows for the synchronous division of the person while disrupting the relation of individual and society. Living beings, plants, things, landscapes or supernatural actors can be regarded as persons, holy crocodiles as well as entire political communities as "collective objects."

With Fortes, however, a diachronous aspect can also be imagined, which understands the person as a development-historical figure growing over the entire course of a life. On this diachronous but not necessarily linear axis, alongside the notion of a person only developing in the course of a lifetime, Fortes also emphasizes the connection of persons with their ancestors. From this view, persons are paradoxically only complete when they enter the succession of ancestors by their own death, thus becoming ancestors themselves. Personhood remains pure potentiality over the whole lifespan. The ancestors "on the other side of the ritual curtain"[2] decide whether a human being has been a person. However, just as Fortes—in this respect in an almost Nietzschean way—defines the person as an effect of morality and lineage, his view of dividual con- and disjunctions over generations tends toward a consideration of origin that is modified by western philosophy: the lineage becomes a collective person, but only to the extent that it expresses the continuation of the founding ancestor in his descendants. It is only at the end of his essay that Fortes mentions an exception to the strict sequence of the patrilinear principle: the descendants of the female line, whose ancestor lived four or five generations before them, live dispersed, not together in the territory of their clan. Their relationship is one of unlimited mutuality beyond codes of conduct determined by territory, beyond the shaping of individuals by morality and the male lineage.

In 1976, in his essay on person and caste in India, "Hindu Transactions: Diversity without Dualism," the US anthropologist McKim Marriott developed not only a "dividualist model of transaction in India," but also concretely introduced the terms "dividual person" and "dividual actor" into the anthropological discussion.[3] He emphasized that persons in South Asia, in contrast to western tradition, are not thought of as individual, inseparable, delimited and therefore limited units, but fundamentally as fluid, only loosely distinguished—dividual. Marriott's ethno-sociological perspective understands the dividual as an interwoven aspect of biological and ethical-juridical instability.

The trans-actional approach, which broadened anthropological theories on barter and exchange in the 1970s, is principally an anti-essentialist attempt to not limit transactions to the exchange of clearly circumscribed things between clearly circumscribed persons. The exchange of animals, shells, food, but also of labor, status and power is to be understood as a transaction between parts of actors and as a transformation of the actors themselves. Transactions thus affect the individual body as internal transformations, but they also traverse persons, bodies and—particularly relevant in the colonial and post-colonial interpretation of the Indian caste system—different castes.

This is a process of absorbing heterogeneous materials that move in and through the persons, and at the same time of releasing "coded substances, essences, residues or other active impacts," which reproduce in others something of the essence of the persons they come from. The interplay of codes and substances is at the core of this process. In the anthropological context codes prove to be codes of conduct that cannot be separated from specific modes of subjec-tivation and self-relations. Substances, on the other hand, contrary to classical concepts of substance, are to be taken as constantly changing and multiple. They can be body parts, organs or bodily fluids, but also cooked food, alcohol or earth, and even alms or knowledge. In processes of becoming parents, marriage, trade, cele-brating and the exchange of services and knowledge, processes of separating and re-composing occur incessantly. The separability of action and actor, of code and substance is, from this perspective, an abstraction of western philosophy. For this reason, Marriott proposes the concept of code/substances or substance/codes: different modes of action and conduct are just as little to be separated from "their" substances as actors from "their" actions. They are embodied by actors, and they become substances in the flow of the things going back and forth between actors.

Embodied substances and codes of conduct mingle in bodies, and at the same time they are completely inseparable from the outside world. What takes place between the actors and what takes place within them are the same processes of mixing and separating. Here dividuality refers—again counter to classical concepts of substance—to the divisibility of substance/codes, to the constant circulation of the substance/code particles, and ultimately to the inevitable transformation of all entities through a constant process of dividing and recombining their substance/codes.[4]

With these theoretical developments of fluidifying codes and substances, the dividual line, in anthropology as well, ends up near discussions marked here by the concept of subsistential division. However, it takes the great leaps between barely comparable social, historical and geopolitical contexts that are significant for anthropological method and often problematic, in this case from West African extensions of personhood across generations to the fluid notions of personhood in the Indian caste system and finally to the exchange of gifts on the Melanesian islands northeast of Australia, in order to arrive at a more in-depth concept of the dividual. In 1988 the feminist anthropologist Marilyn Strathern frames a conceptual invention in her introduction to *The Gender of the Gift*,[5] which allows the philosophy of dividuality to crystallize beyond previous anthropological approaches in a theoretically complex ethnological work. Without essentializing Melanesia as a pre-capitalist outside, without obscuring the colonial and postcolonial overcodings in her field, Strathern succeeds in describing Melanesian personhood in contrast to the externalized relationship of the individual with things in possessive individualism—as divided and composed, permeated by social relations and collected by things, vulnerable and divisible.

The first fundamental precondition for Strathern's field studies in the western highlands of Papua New Guinea is the problematization of the classic western antinomy of society and individual.[6] Strathern begins her introduction on "anthropological strategies" with the ironic remark that "scholars trained in the western tradition cannot really expect to find others solving the metaphysical problems of western thought."[7] For those not from this tradition, it would be equally absurd to focus their philosophical energies on issues such as the relationship between the individual and society as an ordering and unifying figure. Presuppositions of the "socialization processes" of single actors or of political activities that necessarily lead to social structures of spatial integration and social control thus prove to be basic components of an occidental-universalistic view. Strathern turns this relationship around, insofar as she begins by interpreting the western world as particular and integrating it into a dual opposition Melanesian/western. At the same time, she does not limit this to a banal reversal along the lines of saying "because 'our' ideas are 'ethnocentric,' we should look at 'their' ideas." To avoid these kinds of simplifications, she always remains primarily interested in the particular western discourses and their unquestioned discursive preconditions.

Yet Strathern's point is not simply to demonstrate the uselessness of this or that specific western concept, thus confirming the antinomy. She crosses the dualism individual–society with two further dualisms and engenders a heterogeneous field of shifted oppositions by overlapping them. In keeping with the title of her book, the first is the dualism of gift economy and commodity economy. Yet gift economy here by no means provides a positive, domination-free counter-image to capitalist, possessive-individualist society. Instead, Strathern is interested in finding out what (gendered) form domination assumes in the gift economy.[8] In addition, there is a third dualism of anthropological and feminist theory, which primarily enables distantiation from anthropological constructs through feminist critique. Strathern emphasizes that this critique is always socially interested and that in this social interest there is an indirect commentary relating to anthropological reductions.

On the whole, this mutually interlacing, layered approach, less intersectional than constantly shifting the dualisms, does not at all imply symmetrical relations, parallels between the single pairs or unexpected compromises. Instead, it creates further complications, such as through the assertion that in the difference between western and Melanesian sociality, western feminist insights cannot simply be extended to the Melanesian case. Counter to the dominant view of the relation of men and women necessarily imagined as hierarchical and controlling in Melanesian sociality, already in the late 1980s Strathern developed a differentiated perspective in a comparison of various studies in different areas of Melanesia. This perspective takes gender into consideration but never considers it unequivocally as a process of subjugation, describing women neither as a "problem" nor one-dimensionally as "victims," but casts men "as a problem for themselves," as it were, in many different ways.

At a central juncture in the introductory chapter Strathern returns to the starting point of her critique, to the totalizing western fixation regarding the relationship of individual and society. Strathern does not abandon the concept of sociality (in contrast to that of society), but, in order to conceptualize the creation and mainte-nance of relationships in the Melanesian context, she insists on a vocabulary that allows sociality to appear in the singular and in the plural at once. And exactly the same twofold possibility exists for personhood, about which she writes:

> Far from being regarded as unique entities, Melanesian persons are as dividually as they are individually conceived.[9]

What is important here is, first of all, the emphasis on the aspect of how they are conceived: this is not a fixed distinction between "individuals" and "dividuals," but rather between a dividual and an individual perspective on persons. In Melanesian socialities persons are understood as the plural and compound site of relationships, through which they are produced. Whereas the individual perspective contrasts the individuals that form the society with the forming of individuals by society—they become (are made into) social beings in society—the dividual perspective already views the single person as a "social microcosm," thus divided and composed.[10]

The complementary counter-image to the dividual personality consists in a sociality, for example, that found in (male) cultic performances, which, though implying a number and being populated by a multiplicity of persons, is nevertheless perceived as a unit. Strathern calls this a "process of depluralization," which has a unifying effect, even though it is evoked by singular events and the abilities and desires of the many. It is not the realization of generalizing and integrative principles that makes the sociality here, but rather the bringing together of a multiplicity of internal homogeneities, at once disparate persons in the collective event. Strathern even goes so far as to characterize the singularities of collective action as amoral and anti-social, in contradistinction to western notions of hierarchic relations also as "self-contained sociality."[11]

She is not content, however, with simply paradoxically reversing the antinomy, addressing what is composite in the individual and what is unified in sociality, which would not change the imputed relation of dominance of one over the other. To avoid this simple reversal, she complicates here as well the relation of composite personality and anti-social unified sociality with a further dimension. She develops two forms (or modes or stages of a bodily process), which are suited to both the plural and the singular: composite and duality.[12] Whereas the plural is internally composite and externally dual, the singular is externally composite and internally dual. The plural group is internally structured by its parts and can externally encounter another group in a dual way. Singularity consists of a whole spectrum of relationships that are objectified and composed by the person, and which reduce their multiplicity to the image of a dual relationship (such as that to the family of the mother, to the family of the father, etc.)

Strathern distinguishes "unmediated relationships," in which persons have a direct physical and mental influence, from "mediated relationships" based on the exchange of objects. In "unmediated relationship" persons do not separate anything from themselves. The effect is direct, they directly affect one another, not via a part passing between them as in the mediated relationship. The capacity of this direct effect of one person on the body and mind of another produces an asymmetry between the two parties. Strathern calls this first mode, somewhat counter-intuitively, an exchange, even part of the "gift exchange."[13] It is precisely this process in the unmediated relationship, affecting without means, which makes it possible to imagine dividuality beyond Maussian and Derridian conceptions of the gift, without the mediating function of the gift. Strathern nevertheless insists on calling this paradoxically gift-less transaction a gift relationship, because the differences between "mediated" and "unmediated relationship" are mutually related, such that it is not possible to think of one without the other.

The classic form of the gift economy remains the "mediated relationship." In ceremonies of exchange and transaction, things and even persons are understood as parts of persons. As parts, things can circulate between persons and "mediate" their relationships. In this respect, objects produce relationships. Yet not only do objects produce relationships: conversely, transactions also produce objects—they even produce persons as objectifications ("personifications") of relationships.[14] Individual subjects turn themselves into persons/objects in the regard of others. They objectify themselves and thus become active agents.

In this context, a gift—regardless whether it is a matter of "mediated" or "unmediated relationships"—is not an object that is given by a subject, whether as *munus*, tribute, sacrifice, moral or economic debt, whether as an amoral gift, obligatory excess, potlatch. The gift is not a giving-away in the sense of a loss for the subject, who either subjects or empowers her/himself in the giving through the act of giving up and giving over. Even though things and persons are involved here, dividual flows do not function through subject-object separations, but rather through dis- and conjunction, dis/associations, particles that are accelerated and others that persist in constraint or stability. This also brings us towards an answer to Strathern's abovementioned central question, regarding the form domination assumed in gift economies. She provides this answer herself at the end of the first part of *The Gender of the Gift*: "In a gift economy, we might argue that those who dominate are those who determine the connections and disconnections created by the circulation of objects."[15] Neither rigidly separated and gendered management of the public and the private nor "bio-moral ranking," as McKim Marriott describes the dividual asymmetries of substances and codes of conduct, is decisive for the question of domination, but rather the closing and opening of the relays that govern the movement of objects.

This flowing relationship does not function in the logic of the patriarchal economy of partition, nor is it a relationship of mediation in the sense of a transfer from one to another with the help of a medium. Instead, this relationship implies a middle that sweeps things as persons and persons as agents along, without means, without medium, without mediation. This middle is a place where things pick up speed or get caught up; it is permeated by asymmetries and hierarchies that are always rearranging themselves. In this sense, Strathern also clarifies that subsistential division and vulnerability are by no means absent in the gift economy: "The person is vulnerable, so to speak, both to the bodily disposition of others towards him or her and to their wills and desires."[16]

In Marilyn Strathern's social anthropological studies, dividuality appears primarily as the dividual-machinic compositeness of personality and sociality. Yet there is also a dividual line, which traverses times, diachronously, across generations, through histories: if the person is composite, permeated by social relationships, a microcosm of relationships, then this is not at all strictly simultaneous. The composite is composed of various memories and references to the past, bodies exhibiting imprints from past encounters. For Strathern this applies primarily to the memory of a vulnerable body, which reveals a series of past events and "becomes thereby composed of the specific historical actions of social others: what people have or have not done to or for one."[17] The authority of the original ancestor and his lineage no longer holds here; complex mixings of diverse dividual lines traverse not only individual bodies and social spaces, but also time-spaces.[18]

[: *Whilst on a smoothed wave A boat, in it with her maid The girl lept for fear Saving her carried her to this shore.* They steal away, flee the domination of partition, subjugation, shipping, enslavement. They are afraid in the expanse, and yet they draw a line into the sea. They divide the expanse of the water with their line. They run out of breath, are drawn further by the line, rowing, *as best they can*, after their line. *It is like a rough sketch of a calming and stabilizing center in the heart of chaos*. The line is never *itself already a skip*: it is not straight, it is irregular, bends, stops and starts again. It divides the chaos, *it jumps from chaos to the beginnings of order in chaos and is in danger* of being blurred, dissolved, *of breaking apart at any moment.*

What's this I see? Two young women sitting in a boat alone. How the poor things are being tossed about. The surge is driving the boat away from the rock towards the shore. Not a helmsman could have ever done it better. They are struggling to calm *the forces of chaos, keep them outside*; they are trying to tame the line and to be cast on land by it. If it goes badly, they will be swallowed by it. If it goes well, the line will spit them out onto land.

The land is no white spot on the map, no *tabula rasa*, no empty space for building sand castles. There are already earthly forces there, "our forces," whose territories are so rigidly partitioned and distributed that "we" can no longer even see this distribution. "At home," partition of "our countries," "our seas," *mare nostrum, terra nostra, Europa nostra*. The Mediterranean today is the continuation of an occidental space of violence, the liquid-solid middle of violence as *mediterraneum*. Yet far more than just the fringes and passages between sea and land, this space stretches into the force centers of the middle, from which violence streams forth even stronger than from the water-graves of the nameless many and from the edges near the water.

The antidote is not the grand narrative, heroic memory of a better time, it must be found in the here and now of the dividual lines, in the molecular pores of everyday life. Return of the leap in space and time, between the present becoming and the past. Stealing away between the forces of chaos, creating new subsistential territories in the gaps and minimal interstices of the cosmic and earthly forces, chaosms, smugglers, *harraga*, flight, *Fluchthilfe*, especially on the deceptively safe ground of the dominant middle of Europe. :]

The Invention of Dividual Law:
Sumak kawsay and the New Subsistential Territories

Law is not necessarily always only a preserving power, handmaid of a force long since constituted, tool of established institutions, instrumental means of a state apparatus. One line of the possible non-servility of law is the broad field of jurisprudence—breaking through its conventional reading as a dependent application of law. This does not operate at the level of concepts like "state under the rule of law" or "universal human rights," but instead achieves a new actuality with each new judgment. In so doing, it by no means moves in the terrain of a sovereignty situated wherever, and yet it goes far beyond the static force of purely safeguarding and reinforcing, of preserving the law. This holds for the decisions of ordinary courts and all the more to the spheres of constitutional court jurisprudence, of informal law, of community law, of truth commissions or of indigenous jurisprudence.

The Eurocentric-colonial genealogy of law inscribes law as part of a servile, striating and striated logic, the logic of property and the primacy of the individual. The preconditions of Eurocentric-juridical discourses include the instance of a responsible and indivisible individual, a *legal* person, who can also assume undivided responsibility by means of their identifiability. Law and property are tied to an individual subject on the one hand, to a territory on the other. This construction of individual rights has not only been seen as the basis of every possible law since modernity, it is also projected backwards onto the laws of antiquity, especially Roman law.

Just as the primacy of the individual extends discursively into the past, it is also supposed to colonize present becoming. Even though ideas about non-anthropocentric law have emerged in recent decades, particularly from a broader ecological perspective, the foundations of these ideas are not distant at all from the fundamental reference to the individual. In developing his theses of *Wild Law*, for instance, the South African environmental lawyer Cormac Dullinan begins by opposing the false dichotomy between the wild and the law, between nature and civilization.[19] His stance, however, remains a deeply universal-humanist one, with a benevolent view of the human being as a good wild being, the good wild animal, the good wild nature. On the other hand, he can imagine including the wild in law only in a process of recognition as a subject. Just as companies, associations and other "legal entities" gain a legal status in the construction of the juridical person following the pattern of the individual, the vague notion that other entities, such as animals, trees, the deceased, divinities, and the earth as a whole, should "have rights" works analogously.[20] Even though some states have made progress in these issues, such as in the context of animal rights, the linear success story of the individual is perpetuated here: as a continuous further expansion of the struggle against exclusion from individuality, initially against slavery as exclusion of the human being (here the temporal parallel of the imposition of colonization and slave trade with the invocation of universal human rights is notable), then against the exclusion of animals, then against the exclusion of other life forms from the individual sphere of law.

Undoubtedly, these first steps in the new terrain of an ecological law in the broadest sense are extremely difficult. In the limited holistic positions on expanding rights, however, the wild remains imprisoned in an organic paradigm (and its new hierarchies, as with Cullinan, such as that of "Great jurisprudence," "Earth jurisprudence" and "species jurisprudence"[21]). Instead of keeping with the orgic-machinic ecology of bodies/spirits, things and socialities, as developed by Félix Guattari in his books *The Three Ecologies* and *Chaosmosis*, this organic paradigm couples a critique of civilization with a superficial critique of capitalism. With "nature" as a universal point of reference and a basic notion that it would be advisable to imitate its orders, the legal position in Cullinan's organic paradigm is shifted simply from object to subject. What eludes this perspective are modes of subjectivation before and beyond identification as individuals, before and beyond the structural analogy to individual law: dividual relationships, machinic concatenations, socialities as primary reference points of law, as well as non-essentialist forms of reference to earth, nature, landscape and territory.

Félix Guattari captured these kinds of references particularly in the concept of the "existential territory." Existential, or better here: subsistential territories are not originary-substantial grounds, they are "territories never given as object but always as intensive repetition, as piercing existential affirmation."[22] Substistential territories are nothing other than ritornellos, which in their repetitions, in their heterogeneous modes of reterritorializing and deterritorializing, constantly redesign and differentiate the territories. The ritornello always carries the earth with it, the *terra* of the territory and the concrete earth, and at the same time it is the ritornello of setting off, of deterritorialization. Dividuality and radical inclusion are not mutually exclusive factors in the subsistential territories.

> It is one and the same thing to declare these territories partial and yet open to the most diverse fields of alterity: this clarifies how the most autistic enclosure can be in direct contact with ambient social constellations and the machinic unconscious, historical complexes and cosmic aporias.[23]

Notions of a dividual law do not imply that the sphere of the dividual and its subsistential territories are paradisiacal landscapes. However, they should also not be disambiguated and equated with processes of domination and disfranchisement, the introduction of conditions of lawlessness, or the governmental informalization of law. Instead, it is necessary to recognize dividuality both as potentially overcoming Eurocentric law in its own terrain and as potential appropriation by this law, as extension of the state apparatus to areas seemingly outside the state.

In his early texts, Boaventura de Sousa Santos already called the informalization of law part of a process of "disorganization on community level":

> What is new in current informalization and community programmes is that while up until now the oppressed classes had been disorganized at the individual level, that is, as citizens, voters, welfare recipients, in the future they will be disorganized at the community level. I suggest that state sponsored community organization will be the specific form of disorganization in late capitalism.[24]

That was in 1980, and with the increasing valorization of informal labor and approaches to order through civil society, up to today's invocations of resilience and "big society," the disorganization steered by the state has reached an incredible magnitude. Santos' text has an anticipatory quality here, including in the way he uses the term of the chaosmic[25] to explain disorganization through informalization:

> To the extent that the state [...] tries in those reforms to integrate the sanctioning power inherent in the ongoing social relationships, it is indeed explicitly connecting its cosmic power to the chaosmic power, which up until now had been outside its reach.[26]

The situation of a clear separation between the cosmic power of the state and the chaosmic power of social relationships turns into an increasingly one-sided subservience: in Santos' Foucauldian (and implicitly Guattarian) interpretation, the over-coding of chaosmic power by the state apparatus is to be understood as an expansion of the state. Informal law is being appropriated. Where the state purports to withdraw, it expands into civil society; what appears to be de-legalization is actually re-legalization.

What is called dividual law here is not intended to trivialize or deny these processes of de- and re-legalization. The following, however, focuses on the emancipatory sides of the developments within law that aim to change its colonial determination and which—as suggested above—are not to be understood as intervention from outside, but rather as immanent movement. A dividual law understood in this way would no longer only be law-destroying, but part of a law-making, chaosmic power at the same time, questioning and attacking given concepts of law, but also making new ways of law. This way of making law would breach dominant law, as the unstriated would repeatedly thwart juridical standards and their components of striation, property and individualization. This would be a law, a constitution, not based on individuals and their property, but rather on the singularity of manifold ecologies beyond property and individualization. A law that would bring "a new constitution for every generation," with Antonio Negri "constituent power" as absolute process, constituent process.[27]

The moment of instituting is virulent for every further moment of constituting. In this sense, dividual law begins with the instituent act of every constituent process, and it makes a crucial difference whether this instituent act is posited by a sovereign representing the numbered mass or is a manifold process of the innumerable many. It is only in the interplay of the forms and contents of law-making that a dividual law can be imagined that is both law-destroying and law-making, attacking the dominant law of individuality and territory as property and inventing new modes of dividual law-making at the same time.

The Latin American experiences of recent decades can be explained as steps toward dividual law. Following the Zapatista revolt in Mexico in 1994, the rebellion of Quito in 1999 and many other social struggles against dictatorship and neoliberal transformation, there were leftist election victories all over the continent, which consequently also resulted in crucial breaks in law-making. When Hugo Chávez won the presidential election in Venezuela in 1998 and took office in February 1999, he initiated elections for a constitutional assembly, which developed the new "Bolivarian Constitution" through an extended procedure of popular debates over the course of one year. Even if the participation and activation of the population are not able to shake off the smell of machinic subservience in any place of machinic capitalism, it was exactly this form of broad involvement that radically opposed the usual forms of representation, such as the instituting of a limited body that is supposed to represent groups of the population and single-handedly draft the text of the constitution. The contents of the new constitution were not only broadly discussed, but in some points even far surpassed conventional constitution texts in their emancipatory potential, including in the areas of women's rights, indigenous rights and environmental rights.[28]

In Ecuador work on the constitution started with the discussions of a constitutional assembly in 2007.[29] The Constituyente convened from November 2007 to July 2008, and its proposal was accepted in September 2008 with nearly 64% of the votes. Here too, the people's involvement was central, and this was particularly so with respect to the social movements. Accordingly, Magdalena León T. locates the two determining traits of the constitution in the "cosmovision and practice of the indigenous peoples" and in the "feminist and ecological economy of recent decades."[30]

It was in the negotiations of the constitutional assembly and the surrounding discourses that a version of the family of terms associated with the indigenous term of *sumak kawsay* appeared for the first time in the context of a constitutional discussion. *Sumak kawsay* describes the principle of a good life and living together in abundance, exchange and intercourse among all living creatures.[31] Based on the indigenous demands for autonomous self-administration (including of justice and economy), the close connection between subsistential territory (as a habitat tracing back to the ancestors and as space of the *pachamama*) and political, legal and economic self-organization becomes apparent here. With a view to limiting the exploitation of natural resources, the material aspect of territory includes not only land (in the sense of legally attributed ownership of land), but also the space and natural resources. Here, subsistential territory also has a temporal component, the chaosmic concatenation of the here and now with what is long past, of present becoming with passing. These temporal concatenations conjoin with immaterial rights all the way to knowledge production, to science and technology as parts of a notion of good life and living together.[32]

There are many forms, in which the link between living together and a non-retrospective form of reterritorialization is manifested in language: *suma qamaña* (*Aymara* in Bolivia), *sumak kawsay* (*Quechua* in Ecuador), *ñande reko* (*Guaraní* in Paraguay), *vivir bien* or *buen vivir* in Spanish are complementary terms emphasizing different aspects. Translating them is difficult, because entire world-views are transported with the terms, which are in turn difficult to render in other languages. Francesco Salvini points out that it may be specifically the untranslatable nuances in the translations *between* the indigenous versions, but also among their European relatives, *sumak kawsay, suma qamaña, la buona vita, el buen vivir,* the beauty of living, which open up a new territory of imagination.[33]

kawsay is not a noun, so it does not mean "life," as for instance in Italian "*la buona vita*," but rather "to live." To live means here primarily living together in the sense of *convivencia*, a non-individual perspective of mental, social and environmental ecologies. The meaning of *sumak* oscillates between good and beautiful, and the adverb is not subordinated to the verb *kawsay*. *sumak kawsay* could also be called the "art of living beautifully."[34] However, this is not a matter of a good, beautiful life in the sense of an individual way of life that follows certain, ever so strict ethical and aesthetic norms. To live beautifully refers instead to *a* life as a singular assemblage of modes of subjectivation, which is at the same time a dividual life, never whole, but always before the whole, before that which is indivisible, undivided (implying the negation of dividing), in manifold exchange with all living beings. "Living beautifully"—the beautiful is not understood here as an adjectival affiliation or subordination, but rather as an adverbial, therefore independent quality. The life that is meant here *is* not simply beautiful, but instead emerges in a beautiful way.

In the Ecuadorian constitution the concept of *sumak kawsay* already appears as a goal of society in the preamble: "We decide to build a new order of cohabitation for citizens, in its diversity and in harmony with nature, to achieve *buen vivir, sumak kawsay.*"[35] This claim is explained in greater detail in further articles as the right to live in a healthy and ecologically balanced environment (Art. 14), as well as with an explicit reference to indigenous justice (Art. 171) and indigenous territorial districts (Art. 257). Even though these legal extensions remain highly contradictory in political reality,[36] indigenous justice and its anchoring in the constitution nevertheless attain the function of that which cannot be wholly captured and measured within a law that is marked by property, territory and individuality.

In a study on the reflection of overlapping practices of state and indigenous justice in Bolivia and Ecuador that he coordinated in 2012, Boaventura de Sousa Santos proposes two central concepts: the first is *interlegalidad*, knowledge that can emerge under certain circumstances in which people are able to decide between two forms of justice. The second proposal is *híbridos jurídicos*, legal terms and procedures that take up aspects from different legal systems. Santos speaks here of a bilinguality in matters of law.[37] Instead of a rigid and mutually exclusive duality of indigenous and state law, what can also emerge here is an *ecología de saberes y de prácticas jurídicas*, a complex ecology of forms of knowledge and juridical practices. In the development of interlegality and juridical hybrids it becomes clear that the figure of the mutual exclusion of dividual and classical law does not hold.[38] Rather the law of indigenous justice potentially shifts the constitution as well as the practice of jurisprudence from the inside, especially in relation to the primacy of the individual. The law of *sumak kawsay* is not simply limited to a continual further expansion of law, classically based on the primacy of the individual, to all human beings and all forms of life beyond humans. It is not civil law, not limited to the citizen, to the human being, to individual living beings. Here, the law no longer depends on the two aspects of property and individuality. Territory is no longer that of land ownership along with its rigid land registry of even past ownership (which also goes hand in hand with capturing the memory of earlier owners). The claim to self-administration of subsistential territory tends to break through the logic of possessive individualism. This break does not just replace the individual with other, collective identities, be they ethnic, national or other group identities, but rather poses the necessity of a law that builds on the between of singular modes of subjectivation, on the middle of dividual ecology.

A dividual ecology takes into consideration the modes of subjectivation (as mental ecology), the between of sociality (as social ecology) and the earth (as ecology of the environment in the narrower sense).[39] This complex accumulation of ecological modalities helps us to go beyond essentialist connotations of nature, earth and cosmos. It is the snares of anthropological exoticism that lead to misinterpreting *sumak kawsay* as an esoteric primitive belief. It is not simply a retrospective movement toward a community of forefathers, an invocation of the soil or other essentialist figures that are the basis of the hybrid and dividual ecology of *sumak kawsay*. When the discourse around *sumak kawsay* refers to a past prior to colonization and subjugation, then this is primarily to emphasize their temporary character. Before this, however, there is the primacy of struggles, the subsistential division and the dividual constitution of the social, historically always mutable and yet ineluctable.

The current fields of struggle necessarily develop from the lines of flight of indigenous, ecological and feminist struggles: monopolist land ownership, extractivism, strategies of displacement and the renewed colonization of im/material commons call for constituting new modes of subjectivation that no longer take recourse to the primacy of the individual. The ecology of *sumak kawsay* emerges, most of all, as the return of the experience of anti-colonial struggles, of decolonial critique, of resistance against colonial genealogies. This return is actualized in the precarious politics of an untimely present that develops the art of living beautifully from the struggles. The present becoming, the extended here and now of *sumak kawsay* is thus by no means without history, but it is also not just the experience of a transition, as it is read in some interpretations of *sumak kawsay* that are close to the state.[40]

The present becoming of *sumak kawsay* emerges on the one hand in the anti-linear leaps that break open the continuum of colonial and even anti-colonial historiography and found other narrations, other assemblages of events, other modes of writing and story-telling. These leaps do not jump at us from the past like zombies, undead spirits demanding satisfaction for the disruption of their eternal rest, and they are also not just "our" leaps, a voluntaristic appropriation of a past that is simply available to us. The return of the leap in time takes place between the times, between present becoming and passing. The leap between the times is not an invocation of great past times, but rather the specific form of the dividual line, prodding backward into the past, a line to ancestors who are not necessarily our ancestors, not a family line, not a lineage, but rather a line to objects belonging to no one, a line to past socialities that provided no grand narratives. Leaps between the times, demonically hopping, never getting stuck, bifurcating, seeking out ever new forms of resistance in what is past and in what is becoming. Becoming-minoritarian in the subsistential territory that promises no grand future, but also does not draw us back and into the linear past of the forefathers, drawing down into the earth of blood and soil.[41]

Immanence, multitude of existential territories, diffusion of dividual law within the code of law: *sumak kawsay* implies that living well also means living beautifully. It brings the measureless all the way into the constitution, but its chaos is a composed and composing chaos. This composition and recomposition corresponds to its emergence from the indigenous forms of struggle and knowledge of the cosmovision and those of the leftist movements of Latin America. The subsistential territories that emerge in today's social struggles also produce the spheres of dividual law, from which new chaosmovisions can grow. Perhaps constituent processes will unfold not only for the Latin American region, but also as an expansion of decolonial critique in the originating geographies of colonialism as well. The passing in the present becoming of *sumak kawsay* then corresponds to that coming specter, which in the raging middle of multiple crises, in search of form and name, is also haunting Europe.

Molecular Revolution and Condividuality

The dividual is not a meta-historical constant. Perhaps there are indications that the concept and its components developed in early Scholasticism may, as the becoming-dividual of production and social relations, specify the tunings and keys of the abstract and revolutionary machines today. It is then a matter of perspective whether the concept of the dividual is disambiguated as a description of the most recent capitalist transformations or it is also regarded as a manifold component of current social struggles which—depending on political and theoretical positioning—precedes capitalist modes of production or engages them in fist fights.

In this multifaceted rising tide of dividualism between new forms of machinic (self-) subjugation and the search for suitable weapons, the problem of concatenation appears all the more urgent. Whereas the component of division may be sufficiently conceptualized in the dividual, there is something missing on the other side, on the side of articulation and organization, the "political composition" of the multitude. Which -with- for the many? Which form, which "co-formity" can the dis-/association of singularities assume, which -with- that is not binding bond, community, *communitas*? How can such a kind of co-formity be envisioned, without deriving it from the one or melting it into one, beyond the alternative of whether the many unfold from the one or strive for the one in keeping with the motto *e pluribus unum*, in an eternal bond of the reference of the one to the many and the many to the one? Which terminology is suitable for a specific form of dis-/association that insists on the component of the singular, the affirmative mode of separating and dividing *and* the components of the composition, the concatenation, the -with-? How can transversal forms of the dis-/association of singularities be imagined and conceptualized, without individually stratifying and/or totalizing singularities? How can this dis-/association elude the sad figures of self-division, separation, sacrifice, debt, diminution? How can dis-/association happen without being degraded into a smoothing lubricant for the transformations of machinic-capitalist modes of production, without accelerating exploitation, domination and subjugation?

Certainly, the multitude has been invoked now for almost two decades. "In truth, it is not enough to say, 'Long live the multiple,' difficult as it is to raise that cry. [...] The multiple *must be made.*" Making the multiple, its division and its -with-, means inventing a now molecular revolution.[42] The components of molecular revolution appear as actualizations of the components of the dividual: once again dispersion, singularity, similarity. Dispersion as an abstract line moving through single things instead of concentrating them as units. Singularity as singular subsistence instead of generalizing many single things in an original or universal substance. Similarity not as a step along the way to leveling, adapting, means to the end of sameness, but rather as a condition of the multi-formed, abstract line that permeates the co-forming.

1. Dispersion, Abstract Line

Subjectless destitution, occupation without subject, asubjective composition. No unity, no subject, no identifiable class. Classic theories of revolution would classify this lack as a problem. The (revolutionary) subject as a condition of the possibility of revolt, insurrection, revolution, as a fixed component of a theory of stages:

from this perspective, it is only when the subject appears on the horizon as a unified subject, as a molar block, as the working class, as a united front, that the revolution can begin.

And yet, the absence of the subject does not have to be interpreted as a deficiency. Quite the opposite, it could indicate a new quality in the revolution, in a henceforth *molecular* revolution, and the primacy of multiplicity within it. When the subject is missing, it has not just gone amiss, as a gap (still) gaping and begging to be closed. The composition of the molecular revolution does not need unification or the representation of a unified (class) subject by leaders, party and vanguard. The rejection of the primacy of *the* class, or of a specific class (be it the "working class," "the precariat" or a middle-class threatened by decline) does not in any way imply tuning out the partition and domination that are taking place more radically than ever in current capitalist production. Machinic capitalism striates the multitude, hierarchizes and valorizes it. And yet molecular revolution raises no hopes in any of the imaginings of resistance against this dividual-machinic capitalism that undertake to homogenize and totalize the multitude. Even in their negative manifestation there is no way back ahead of multiplicity, but only its dis/continuous unfolding.

The point is not an absolute deterritorialization in which every reterritorialization, including attempts at organizing, would remain barred. It is rather a case of molecular forms of organization, of the institution of ever new subsistential territories that are able to counter the closure, unification, machinic subservience and valorization. Instead of accepting the molar organizational narratives of revolutionary history (and its structuralizing historiography) as the only one possible and reproducing it to infinity, there is a need for invention and multiplication of revolutionary practices and narratives. Then, the single great event becomes an unending chain of instituent practices, the overtaking of the state apparatus becomes a consolidation of constituent power, the institutionalization of the revolution becomes the invention of ever new monster institutions.

Dispersion, distributedness, dissipation already exist quite obviously in the contemporary modes of production of machinic capitalism, in current ways of living, in current modes of subjectivation. The multitude has become the technical composition of post-Fordist production, but not only in the obvious sense of individual production in dispersion, in new forms of global home-working, for instance, whether they are "material" or "immaterial." Marx's small-holding peasants as potatoes in a potato sack certainly provide a good image for the aspect of monadic techniques in production. Yet the machinic production-monads are by no means without communication or unable to communicate just because they are dispersed. On the contrary, they have to communicate in order to survive.

The notion of dispersed production is also too static, so long as it is viewed solely as an international distribution of labor and as a distribution of production sites all over the planet. At the same time and alongside this, there is an only seemingly opposite tendency to increasingly placeless or nomadic production. This applies not only to actors of global (financial) management, but rather to a continuum that covers project work and labor migration as well as extreme conditions of fleeing from slavery, violence, war, and from new forms of radical exploitation.

Dispersion and absolute deterritorialization of cooperation remain only unconnected fragments of an interpretation of contemporary production, as long as the perspective remains limited to individuals and their communication. It is not individual actors and their cooperation that are at the center of these modes of production, but increasingly the abstract-dividual lines that traverse the individuals. Dividuality implies dividedness, but neither in relation to individual parts nor to an imagined whole of their community. It is not the separatedness of the whole single things, but rather a distribution, spread, dispersion that extends all the way through various single things. The dividual emerges in drawing the abstract line that traverses and concatenates the concrete single things. The line is abstract insofar as it tears the subsistential territories and particles away from the individual-holistic concretion and connects them at the same time. The separated, subsistential components of the dividual, distributed across various individuals, assemble along the abstract-dividual line.

Whereas dispersion, multitude and cooperation have prevailed at the level of modes of production in the form of a dividual communism of capital, the multiplicity of political organizations has seemed to lag behind in recent decades, as though the old forms of political composition have hindered a non-identitarian composition of the dispersed multitude. Certainly, trade unions, parties and other traditional institutions in their rigid, structuralized form often constitute baits and impediments to the imagination and invention of a molecular political organization. Yet in the shadow of the erosion of socialism, social democracy, welfare state and liberal democracy, practices that are critical of representation and identity are multiplying, decentral, polycentral, molecular ways of organizing. There are more and more local experiences of molecular reterritorialization, its constituent and instituent power, and the impact of these experiences ranges all the way to the invention of new forms of institution. The dividual-abstract line increasingly spreads right through the social movements. It does not expand through the mediation of parties and media, or through a traditional process of internationalization, but instead appears in different places at the same time, translocally, all across the dispersed places.

What applies to the dividual dispersion in space also applies to the alinear, dividual line in time. Current social movements are undoubtedly permeated by genealogical lines of earlier movements and revolts. However, the amphibian paths of the revolutionary machines no longer need any mole burrows today to dig their way through the world and pop up here or there, in different geo-political situations, in old-new form. They do not even need the form of the snake that makes its way to all sides anew, without building a fixed system of tunnels, without limiting itself to one element of the earth and without leaving traces. And yet the manifold components of social struggles return again, as an alinear, singular return of dividual knowledge. Gestural techniques of the social forum, old anarchist modes of action, grassroots-democratic forms of assembly, the human microphone, swarming forms of demonstrations, techniques of horizontality, autonomous practices of occupying buildings, apartments, squares and media, all of these are in no linear relation that would suggest an origin here or there. There are only similarities, recombinations, implicit and explicit references, translation processes in all directions, and productive mistranslations in all dimensions.

2. Singular Subsistences and Becoming-More

In no way does the dividual govern only modes of production and political organization in the narrower sense, as a technical composition that must merely become a political composition. The dividual lines of the molecular revolution traverse ways of living, modes of subjectivation, singular subsistences. Molecularity means the pores of everyday life, transformation of the molecules of sociality, revolutionary transversing of things instead of universality. If the dividual is in diverse single things, then it does not oppose the individual one-sidedly as a universal. It breaks through the dichotomy of the individual and the universal-communitarian, introducing a new dimension, in which the parts of a not-whole are posited in a non-universal, transversal relationship. Dividual abstraction is no generalizing separation, separatedness, disjunction from the concrete, but rather an abstraction as conjunctive disjunction. A molecular organization of singularity does not mean: How do I get the potatoes in a potato sack to communicate?

It would be wrong to explain the emergence and spread of multiplicity in the logic of counting through addition and quantitative multiplication. Producing multiplicity means overcoming the additive logic of counting as well as rejecting the one that first emerges in the counting (off) of multiplicity. The subject, the one, the whole, where it is no longer absent, is not the consequence of a process of collecting, forming, unifying the many, the singular, the dispersed, to be composed into a molar block. The one emerges only when the logic of counting, classifying and identifying lays its grids on multiplicity; when the uncountable is domesticated in the process of counting. The subject can only appear in the minus, the diminution, the subtraction from multiplicity.

If the logic of representation and identity is rejected, if no demands are made, if the primacy of the face and the name are declined, if facelessness and namelessness are proclaimed, if no intellectuals or party secretaries are established as voices of the movement, no visibility in the mainstream media and social media, the problem of propagation remains, and with it the old question: How can there be more of us? The question is put wrong to begin with. Starting out with a We, we always end up with the question of majority. Being-more as majority is the wishful thinking and target point of a propagation imagined in a linear way via sender and receiver, knowledge production and reception, representatives and represented. It is only by turning from the question of majority and being-more to that of becoming-more that the dominant logic of representation and identification can be turned.

Becoming-more always takes place in the dimensions of multiplicity. The majority has no role to play in these dimensions. Multiplication and propagation are not to be understood here as the addition of one individual to another, but, first of all, in the mode of the dividual-machinic. This is where media lose their quality as the center in a linear process of representation from production to reception. It is no longer a question of target-group objects to be "addressed" through mass media with the greatest possible outreach and their author-subjects. The dividual middle is multiplicity itself. Multiplicity does not grow from the root, but from the stem, and it grows out. Here, media are not just a means, they are part of production of sociality, they become social media in a new sense. These forms of social media defy any simple instrumentalization as couplings between active and passive, production and reception. They are technopolitical dispositives, which radically expand the possibilities of mediality and sociality in a self-organized way.

Becoming-more means radical inclusion: by no means the indiscriminate, farcical repetition of a hippie dream, a romantic projection of the suspension of class boundaries and national borders, the fantasy of smooth fraternization. At the same time, the concept does not draw the simple picture of an open door (as in "leaving the door open ajar"), of letting someone into a room and engaging with the one thus admitted, of a possible integration into an already existing territory. Radical inclusion means rather the potentiality of openness of the subsistential territory itself, of a fundamentally inclusive territory without doors or thresholds, not surrounded or traversed from the outset by borders, an inclusive mode of reterritorialization of space and time. This implies not only the break with every social preformation of the territory, but also the impossibility of linear-strategic planning, unpredictability, the social and organizational openness of molecular reterritorialization.

Radical inclusion implies bearing and affirming asymmetries, continuously differentiating and multiplying within them, in a continuous expansion of multiplicity: asymmetry between the differentially hierarchized precarious, manifold geopolitical asymmetry, asymmetry between different groups of homeless, people threatened by homelessness and those fighting for their right to a place to live, asymmetry between the militant modes of expression between younger and older generations, asymmetry between those who can be physically present at an assembly and those who cannot, whose presence however is made possible by a post-media ecology of live streams, tweets and social networks. Finally, radical inclusion in no way implies allowing any reterritorialization in the form of racisms or sexisms. On the contrary, multiplicity is to propose co-forms that deprive any discriminatory identification of its breeding ground.

3. Similarity and Co-formity and Con-dividuality

If the dividual is conceptually determined by dividedness, how does the non-universal concatenating function of dividuality come about? How do division and concatenation, abstraction and concretion relate to one another? Which principle determines the traversals of the abstract line? The key to these questions lies in a complex understanding of similarity and co-formity, through which the molecular revolution becomes a condividual revolution. -with-.

Machinic capitalism modulates and takes into service the atomic level of individual desires for self-division, but it also arranges the molecular level of dividual desiring into new compliant assemblages.

This occurs around the problematic tipping point of similarity. Similarity can be negotiated under the aspect of being-of-the-same-kind, or under the aspect of multiplicity. On the one hand, it can thus serve as an instrument of measurement, adapting and assimilating the parts, as a precondition for translating into quantity, measuring, adapting and leveling the multitude. On the other hand, under the aspect of multiplicity, it can also effect an excess of con-/disjunction that cannot be leveled. In the latter mode, similarity does not serve as a step along the way to adapting and complying with measurement, but rather to becoming incomparable in drawing the line. Conducting no conduct, fitting no fate, forming no form. The non-sensuous, incomprehensible, incompliant similarities cannot be assembled on a straight, adapting, leveling line. They emerge in the breaks, leaps, tensions, in the disbanding of bonds, the delinearization of the line.

The dividual line conjoins what is similar/co-forming in the most diverse single things, but also affirms their separation at the same time. The parts of the dividual line, its components are, following Gilbert, "co-forming, not only although, but because they are diverse," yet they are no longer only different in number. Incompliancy and co-formity are not mutually exclusive, but mutually conditional. Co-formity is form-multiplicity. It implies dividual orientation to the specific resonance but not consonance of the form. Co-formity is, at the same time, multi-formity, orgic form of organization of the molecular revolution. Immeasurable organization instead of formlessness, tipping into multiplicity instead of conforming, co-forming of the endlessly many organizational forms of the non-compliant instead of formalisms and method-fetishisms.

In the struggles against partition and participation, in the proximity zones of division, finally a fourth mode flashes up, a sub-sistential self-dispersion that disquiets rigid order, property and territory. Leaping, erratic, alinear and nevertheless in the potentiality of concatenation, orgic modes of division permeate the unifying mechanisms of organic participation, and condividuality disturbs the truly participating. Nothing is related to the whole, multiplicity moves with singularities. Nothing is partition, limiting and detaching the parts. Dis- and conjunction inhere to condividuality. When the -with- of the faltering and raging middle joins with the dividual, then a concept for the concatenation of singularities emerges, which not only names but also impels their leaps and their assemblies, con/division.

[: Ritornello 9: Now-Time.
Which Animal for a Present Becoming? :]

[: *On the thread* of a line, *one launches forth* from the castle, is drawn out, *hazards an improvisation. But the circle is not opened,* the gates are not passed through, the walls are not moved. The child leaves the territory without stepping over its boundaries. It flies. Absolute deterritorialization without being seen, flying invisibly. Only in the places where the child returns from the mode of absolute smoothness into the subsistential territory, at the thresholds between imperceptibility and perceptibility, at the transitions from flight to earth, there the child must take care.

Yet the child is not alone: the crowd of Berts, Jeannies, Scotties, and Shelmerdines accompanies it, molecular lightweight aircraft, genies from a bottle without a bottle, winged tricycles, double-deckers, airships without helium, enchanting quantum teleportations. Under the radar of the molar, some inhabited by living creatures, some unmanned and therefore no less social drones. They spot the movements of the police, carry those fleeing, sneak through and run, smuggle secret messages into unknown lands.

And they move through the air, some lightly and quietly, others with stuttering engines and all too easily perceived. Swimming moles, flying snakes, animal-machines traversing the elements, undulating all the way through everything. And they not only move through many elements, their aggregate states are also many. Liquid, firm machines, gases. Whirlpool, earthquake, tornado. Scissors, paper, rock.

Dissemblage. :]

Notes

I. DIVIDUUM

1. *Thesaurus linguae Latinae*, Vol. 5.1, 1611f.

2. Although I use the phrase "bce: before common era," rather than "BC: Before Christ," this still holds a clerical and Eurocentric constant that is too little questioned, if at all. Especially in reference to the "before" as an indication of an all-encompassing, homogeneous re-territorialization, this constant is a postulate that colonizes not only space, but also time. At the time of Plautus and Terence, years were counted *ab urbe condita*, starting from the founding of the city of Rome, a mythical beginning similar to the birth of Christ.

3. Roman law did not consider even the rape of a female slave as a violation of her physical integrity, but rather as damage to the property of her lord. Cf. Jane F. Gardner, *Women in Roman Law and Society*, London: Routledge 1987, 166. The ideological foundation was provided by Greek philosophy, for instance Plato, who declared the necessary separation of free people and slaves in the *Laws*, or Aristotle, who described slaves as "animated tools" in the *Nicomachean Ethics*. Roman law (Ulpian Dig. 50,17,32,0) declared slaves to be things, and it was only with Varro/Columella that aspects of good government, positive incentives, more subtle motivation of slaves first appeared, particularly in the sense of enhancing efficiency. Yet this transition is not to be understood as a progressive development in the direction of tolerance and self-government either, but rather as an up-and-down, a simultaneity of different relations of power and domination.

4. Cf. Rolf Friedrich Hartkamp, *Von leno zu ruffiano: Die Darstellung, Entwicklung und Funktion der Figur des Kupplers in der römischen Palliata und in der italienischen Renaissancekomödie*, Tübingen: Narr 2004, 12.

5. On the figure of Labrax, cf. ibid., 97–113. It would also be interesting to investigate the significance of the "panderer" figure for the development of anti-Semitic stereotypes.

6. Cf. Gardner, *Women in Roman Law and Society*, 167.

7. Cf. Peter P. Spranger, *Historische Untersuchungen zu den Sklavenfiguren des Plautus und Terenz*, Stuttgart: Steiner 1984, 64–69.

8. On the figure of Sannio, cf. Hartkamp, *Von leno zu ruffiano*, 144–159.

9. Cf. the reading of exodus that Isabell Lorey has presented in her study of the plebeian secessions. This massive and mass form of flight and exodus also reveals the potential for intervention of constituent power into constituted orders. Isabell Lorey, *Figuren des Immunen. Elemente einer politischen Theorie*, Berlin/Zürich: Diaphanes 2011.

10. The right to asylum that sanctioned legitimate forms of flight in late Roman law (Ulpian, Dig. 21,1,17,12–13) also introduces the problematic distinction in this sanction between the regulation of the *fugitivus*, in other words the illegally fleeing person, and the exception of legal flight because of abuse, etc.

11. Stefano Harney / Fred Moten, *The Undercommons. Fugitive Planning & Black Study*, Wivenhoe / New York / Port Watson: Minor Compositions 2013, 139.

12. The young Karl Marx, in his polemic against Cicero and Plutarch, would in turn later describe the "smithy of the world" as a "noisy affair," an "uproarious contest," a "hostile tension." Cf. Karl Marx, "Notebooks on Epicurean, Stoic and Skeptical Philosophy": https://marxists.anu.edu.au/archive/marx/works/1839/notebook/ch04.htm

13. For a critical edition of the Boethius commentaries, cf. Nikolaus M. Häring, *The Commentaries on Boethius by Gilbert of Poitiers*, Toronto: Pontifical Institute of Mediaeval Studies 1966. For philosophical introductions to the context and the main theses of Gilbert, cf. Bruno Maioli, *Gilberto Porretano. Dalla grammatica speculativa alla metafisica del concreto*, Roma: Bulzoni 1979; John Marendon, "Gilbert de Poitiers," in: Peter Dronke, *A History of Twelfth Century Western Europe*, Cambridge University Press 1992, 328–352; Klaus Jacobi, "Einzelnes— Individuum—Person. Gilbert von Poitiers' Philosophie des Individuellen," in: Jan A. Aertsen / Andreas Speer (Eds.), *Individuum und Individualität im Mittelalter*, Berlin/New York: de Gruyter 1996, 3–21; Luigi Catalani, *I Porretani. Una scuola di pensiero tra alto e basso Medioevo*, Turnhous: Brepols 2008; Luisa Valente, "Un realismo singolare: forme e universali in Gilberto di Poitiers e nella Scuola Porretana," in: *Documenti e studi sulla tradizione filosofica medievale* 19, 2008, 191–246. For a detailed introduction to Gilbert's texts and contexts, cf. Lauge Olaf Nielsen, *Theology and Philosophy in the Twelfth Century: A Study of Gilbert Porreta's Thinking and the Theological Expositions of the Doctrine of the Incarnation during the Period 1130–1180*, Leiden: Brill 1982, especially 25 ff. For a more precise interpretation of Gilbert's Boethius commentaries, cf. Martin Schmidt, *Gottheit und Trinität*, Basel: Verlag für Recht und Gesellschaft 1956.

14. His controversial positions on church politics and his complex, sometimes rather dark argumentation resulted in massive hostility toward Gilbert over the course of centuries (cf. Häring, *The Commentaries on Boethius by Gilbert of Poitiers*, 8). The *Allgemeine Geschichte der christlichen Religion und Kirche* by August Neander introduced him still in 1845 as a "man of unclear, confused, abstruse manners of explanation" (August Neander, *Allgemeine Geschichte der christlichen Religion und Kirche*, Vol. 10, Gotha: Perthes 1845, 899).

15. For the sake of better comprehensibility—and using Gilbert's own mode of expression—in the following I translate *quo est / quibus sunt* as subsistence(s) and *quod est / quae sunt* as subsisting(s).

II. DIVISION

1. Regarding division in Plato cf. the essay "Reversing Plato" by Gilles Deleuze, first published in French in 1967 in the *Revue de métaphysique et de morale*, in English translation and with an introduction by Heath Massey as Appendix 2 in Leonard Lawlor, *Thinking through French Philosophy: The Being of the Question* (Bloomington & Indianapolis: Indiana University Press, 2003), pp. 163–177. Central lines of argument from this essay are taken up in *Difference and Repetition*, trans. Paul Patton (New York/NY: Columbia University Press, 1994), pp. 59–69, and in 1969 in revised form under the title "Plato and the Simulacrum" as an appendix to *The Logic of Sense*, trans. Mark Lester with Charles Stivale (London: The Athlone Press, 1990), pp. 253–266. Regarding the term of the "true participant" cf. Deleuze, *Difference and Repetition*, p. 61.

2. As in Roberto Esposito, *Communitas*, trans. Timothy Campbell, Stanford: Stanford University Press 2010.

3. Michael Hardt and Antonio Negri attempt in *Commonwealth* (Cambridge/Massachusetts: Harvard University Press 2009) to argue against this lineage of the common. As the two authors write in the introduction, on the one hand the common is the name for "the common wealth of the material world— the air, the water, the fruits of the soil, and all nature's bounty—which in classical European political texts is often claimed to be the inheritance of humanity as a whole." On the other hand the common encompasses "all those results of social production that are necessary for social interaction and further production, such as knowledges, languages, codes, information, affects, and so forth" (VIII). In this second view, the common means the practices of interaction, of care, of living together in a common world. These are practices that do not allow for human beings to be understood as separate from nature, neither in the logic of exploitation nor in that of protection. This is where a conceptual tie is found to the line of the commons, which allows for the sharing of the common to be understood not as a becoming-less, but rather as an excess. Throughout the entire book, alongside the two conventional aspects of the common explained in the introduction, a third aspect is also evident, which addresses the question of the concatenation of singular streams: the common as the self-organization of social relationships. This instituting of the common implies that it can be understood not as a being-common, but rather only as a becoming-common, as excessive production of the common, as co-emergence of the singularities and the common. Nevertheless, I remain skeptical in this case as well: what is still missing in the common—as in the entire family of concepts of *communitas*—is the aspect of the many, of their division and their singularity. To express sharing *and* division, to subvert the identitarian and reductive turn of the community, Hardt and Negri's

theoretical tradition is in need of the conceptual composition and connection between common and multitude.

4. Jean-Luc Nancy, "The Confronted Community," Andrew J. Mitchell and Jason Kemp Winfree (Ed.), *The Obsessions of Georges Bataille: Community and Communication*, State University of New York Press 2009, p.24–25

5. See the detailed explanation in Isabell Lorey, *Figuren des Immunen*, Zürich/Berlin: Diaphanes 2011, 181–228.

6. Maurice Blanchot's *The Unavowable Community* (trans. Pierre Joris, Barrytown: Station Hill Press 1988), published in 1983 in dialogue with Jean-Luc Nancy as a critical reflection on the works of Georges Bataille on community, is determined by this figure of community that "arises" in "its communion" (7). Although Blanchot recognizes the necessity of naming the paradoxical bond of singularities in their unboundedness, instead of the suspension of differences in a higher and universal unity, he can only understand this bond as something negative—and there is resonance here with the figure of the *munus* as an obligatory, indebting tie. This is why he writes so much about insufficiency, incompleteness, impossibility, absence, unrepresentability, inadequacy, unavowability in his writing about community. "Abandonment" is needed, the "sacrifice" that first founds the community (15). These figures of deficiency and diminution culminate explicitly in Bataille's and Blanchot's formulation of the "negative community" as a "community of those who have no community" (24).

7. I use Foucault's concept of pastoral power and that of pastoral government in a broader sense, which also leads to the phenomena that Foucault called governmentality and biopower. What is important here is, first of all, that the *pastor*, the shepherd, leads the entire herd and the individuals, secondly that this form of government produces individuals, and thirdly guides them to self-government. The aspect of leading all and each individual at the same time implies a more complex concept than that of the herd in Plato's *The Statesman*, where herd and individuals are considered as opposites. What especially interests me is not the perspective of the governor, but rather that of the governed governing themselves.

8. Recognizing the compatibility of dividuation and individuation in pastoral power ultimately also sheds some light on the solitary and dark statement by Novalis, who wrote as early as 1798/99 in the sentence No. 952 of *Das allgemeine Brouillon*: "Das ächte Dividuum ist auch das ächte Individuum." ("The true dividual is also the true individual.")

9. In one of his last interviews, Foucault thus responded to the question of whether his most recent books were not about a new genealogy of morals: "Notwithstanding the solemnity of the title and the grandiose mark that Nietzsche has left on it, I'd say yes." ("An Aesthetics of Existence," trans. Alan Sheridan, in Michel Foucault, *Politics, Philosophy, Culture*, New York: Routledge 1988, 48)

10. Michel Foucault, *The History of Sexuality, Volume 2: The Use of Pleasure*, trans. Robert Hurley, New York: Vintage Books 1990, 13. In the last part of the introduction to this book there is a more precise description of which forms and relations of "morality and practice of the self" are to be distinguished (ibid., 25–32).

11. Ibid., 28.

12. Ronald D. Laing, *The Divided Self. An Existential Study in Sanity and Madness*, London: Penguin Books 2010 (1960), here 42.

13. Judith Butler, *Precarious Life. The Powers of Mourning and Violence*, London/New York: Verso 2004, 20.

14. Isabell Lorey, *State of Insecurity. Government of the Precarious*, London/New York: Verso 2015; cf. also the reflections of the Madrid feminist collective Precarias a la Deriva on the "Right to Care and Be Cared For" ("A Very Careful Strike—Four Hypotheses," trans. Franco Ingrassia and Nate Holdren, caring labor: an archive (2005), available at "https://caringlabor.wordpress.com/" \ https://caringlabor.wordpress.com.)

15. Lorey, 12, cf. also 17–20.

16. Laing, *The Divided Self*, 49.

17. Félix Guattari, who described Laing himself as "divided" in a small text from 1972, sees a revolutionary in him on the one hand, "when he breaks with psychiatric practice," but on the other hand sees him as still tied to familial postulates that lead to the revelation of a true self as a means of healing: "His search for a 'schizogenius' will never escape from the personological 'nexus'." Félix Guattari, "The Divided Laing," in: ibid., *The Guattari Reader*, ed. Gary Genosko, Oxford: Blackwells 1996, 37–40, here 39; cf. also Gilles Deleuze/Félix Guattari, *Anti-Oedipus*, translated from the French by Robert Hurley, Mark Seem, and Helen R. Lane, Minneapolis: University of Minnesota Press 1983, 362.

18. Laing, *The Divided Self*, 49.

19. Ibid.

III. DIVIDEND

1. Gilles Deleuze, "Postscript on the Societies of Control," in: *Negotiations*, Columbia University 1997, pp.177–182, here: 180. For a current adaptation of these sequences, cf. also Tiziana Terranova, "Red stack attack! Algorithms, Capital and the Automation of the Common," EuroNomade 2014, http://www.euronomade.info/?p=2268.

2. I share the concept of machinic capitalism and its genealogical lines (Marx's machine fragment, its post/operaist development, and especially Félix Guattari's theory of the machinic) with Matteo Pasquinelli (cf. for instance, "Machinic Capitalism

and Network Surplus Value: Notes on the Political Economy of the Turing Machine":
"http://matteopasquinelli.com/docs/Pasquinelli_Machinic_Capitalism.pdf
"\http://matteo-pasquinelli.com/ docs/Pasquinelli_Machinic_Capitalism.pdf), but I
do not want to place the concept in the context of the theoretical current of
accelerationism. Mistaking the resistive affirmation of specific, indeterminate
lines of flight in the field of immanence of contemporary forms of capitalism on
the one hand with the naïve optimism of a generalized acceleration and overcoming of capitalism on the other is based not only on a misunderstanding in
reference to the aforementioned theoretical foundations of the machinic, but also
on simplifying notions of the linearity of history and the absolute deterritorialization
of time. See also the critique by Franco "Bifo" Berardi: "L'accelerazionismo in
questione dal punto di vista del corpo," in: Matteo Pasquinelli (Ed.), *Gli algoritmi
del capitale. Accelerazionismo, macchine della conoscenza e autonomia del commune*,
Verona: ombre corte 2014, 39–43.

3. Harney/Moten, *Undercommons*, 88.

4. Original Facebook slogan, which is still present in the German translation:
"http://www.facebook.com/" (http://de-de.facebook.com/).

5. Michel Foucault, *The History of Sexuality, Volume 1: An Introduction*, translated
from the French by Robert Hurley, New York: Pantheon Books 1978, 60.

6. Ibid., 44.

7. Ibid., 45.

8. Ibid., 60.

9. Felix Stalder, "Autonomy and Control in the Era of Post-Privacy":
http://felix.openflows.com/node/143

10. Foucault, *The History of Sexuality, Volume 1*, 62.

11. Gilles Deleuze, Félix Guattari, *A Thousand Plateaus. Capitalism and Schizophrenia*, translated by Brian Massumi, Minneapolis: University of Minnesota Press
1987, 341.

12. Ibid., 342.

13. Deleuze, "Postscript on the Societies of Control," 180 ["Les individus sont
devenus des ‚dividuels,' et les masses, des échantillons, des données, des marchés
ou des '*banques.*'"].

14. Ibid., 182.

15. Ibid.

16. Stefano Harney, "Istituzioni algoritmiche e capitalismo logistico," in Matteo
Pasquinelli (Ed.), *Gli algoritmi del capitale. Accelerazionismo, macchine della
conoscenza e autonomia del comune*, Verona: ombre corte 2014, 116–129.

17. Ibid., 121.

18. Christian Marazzi, *The Violence of Financial Capitalism*, translated from Italian by Kristina Lebedeva and Jason Francis Mc Gimsey, Los Angeles: Semiotext(e) 2011, 56f.

19. Harney, "Istituzioni algoritmiche e capitalismo logistico," 125f.

20. Randy Martin, *Knowledge LTD: Toward a Social Logic of the Derivative*, Philadelphia: Temple University Press 2015, 61.

21. Harney/Moten, *Undercommons*, 87–99.

22. Cf. Nassim Nicolas Tayeb's concept of "white" and "black swans" (the former stands for the exact occurrence of perfect prediction, the latter for the ideal condition of the improbable) in ibid., *The Black Swan: The Impact of the Highly Improbable*, New York: Random House 2007.

23. Cf. Elie Ayache, *The Blank Swan. The End of Probability*, Hoboken: Wiley 2010.

24. Harney/Moten, *Undercommons*, 92f.

25. Angela Mitropoulos, *Contact and Contagion. From Biopolitics to Oikonomia*, Wivenhoe/New York/Port Watson: Minor Compositions 2012, 216.

26. Arjun Appadurai, "The Wealth of Dividuals in the Age of the Derivative," unpublished manuscript distributed in the context of a larger collective project on *The Wealth of Societies*. Thanks to Arjun Appadurai and Randy Martin for making the manuscript available.

27. Ibid.

28. Brigitte Young, "Die Subprime-Krise und die geschechtsspezifische Schulden-falle," in: *Antworten aus der feministischen Ökonomie auf die globale Wirtschafts-und Finanzkrise*, Berlin: Ebert Stiftung 2009, 15–25, here 25.

29. Appadurai, "The Wealth of Dividuals in the Age of the Derivative."

30. Cf. Martha Poon (quoted in Marazzi, *The Violence of Financial Capitalism*, 36), who describes the actors in the "course of production" of derivatives as "brokers of real estate loans, directly in contact with consumers, the intermediaries who buy wholesale and bring together credit aggregates in accordance with the specifications of financial institutions and hedge funds that, at the end of the line, provide capital, and, finally rating agencies that determine whether the composition of these asset portfolios satisfies their criteria of quality."

31. Marazzi, *The Violence of Financial Capitalism*, 27f. and 56.

32. Ibid., 49.

33. Appadurai, "The Wealth of Dividuals in the Age of the Derivative."

34. Translator's note: the rare German word *eineln* (to unify, to make one) is related to the word *ähneln* (to be similar to), indicating the relation between unifying on the one hand and *similis*, similar and assimilation on the other.

35. Michel Foucault, "Theatrum Philosophicum," translation, by Donald F. Brouchard and Sherry Simon, first published in: *Critique* 282 (1970), pp. 885–908: http://www.generation-online.org/p/fpfoucault5.htm

36. Martin, *Knowledge LTD*, 60.

37. Marazzi, *The Violence of Financial Capitalism*, 40.

38. Ibid. 41f.

39. Cf. Ada Colau / Adrià Alemany, *Mortgaged Lives (From the Housing Bubble to the Right to Housing)*, Los Angeles/Leipzig/London: Journal of Aesthetics & Protest Press 2014.

40. Marazzi, *The Violence of Financial Capitalism*, 95. On this see also Tiziana Terranova, "Red Stack Attack!," who proposes the term Red Stack as a program for the "invention of constituent social algorithms" and socio-technical innovation at the three levels of virtual money, social networks and bio-hypermedia.

41. On the multiple meaning of debt, cf. Deleuze, "Postscript on the Societies of Control," 181: "A man is no longer a man confined, but a man in debt."; the study, building on Marx, Nietzsche, and Deleuze/Guattari, by Maurizio Lazzarato, *The Making of Indebted Man*, translated from French by Joshua David Jordan, Los Angeles: Semiotext(e) 2012, and Randy Martin, "Mobilizing Dance. Toward a Social Logic of the Derivative," in: Gerald Siegmund/Stefan Hölscher (Eds.), *Dance, Politics & Co-Immunity*, Zurich/Berlin: diaphanes 2013, 211: "[...] the social entailments of indebtedness are the basis of political engagement."

42. Harney/Moten, *Undercommons*, 61.

43. Mitropoulos, *Contract and Contagion*, 228.

44. Ibid., 209.

45. Ibid., 216.

46. Ibid., 229.

47. Cf. (also for the following), Martin, *Knowledge LTD*, 52.

48. Ibid., 78.

49. Ibid., 76.

50. Ibid., 75.

IV. CONDIVISION

1. Meyer Fortes, "On the concept of the person among the Tallensi," in: Roger Bastide / Germaine Dieterlen (Eds.), *La notion de personne en Afrique noire. Acte du Colloque international du CNRS*, 544. Paris, Octobre 1971, Paris: L'Harmattan 1973, 238–319. Republished in: ibid., *Religion, Morality, and the Person, Essays on Tallensi Religion*, Cambridge: Cambridge University 1987, 247–286. Deleuze and Guattari refer to Fortes both in *Anti-Oedipus* (146) and in *A Thousand Plateaus* (209 and 212).

2. Fortes, "On the concept of the person among the Tallensi," 285.

3. McKim Marriott, "Hindu transactions: diversity without dualism," in: Bruce Kapferer (Ed.), *Transaction and Meaning. Directions in the Anthropology of Exchange and Symbolic Behavior*, Philadelphia: Institute for the Study of Human Issues 1976, 109–142, here 109.

4. Ibid., 110. Marriott also points out a problematic fourth aspect, which tends to undermine his anti-essentialist interpretation of substance/codes: in Indian thinking it is often explicit that what Marriott calls substance/codes goes back to a certain origin or seeks to reach a certain goal. The problem in this case seems not the western perspective of the lineage, but rather its Indian tradition.

5. Marilyn Strathern, *The Gender of the Gift*, Berkeley/Los Angeles: University of California 1988.

6. Cf. also Strathern's concise and clear representation of this antinomy in: Tim Ingold (Ed.), *Key Debates in Anthropology*, London/New York 1996, 50–55.

7. Strathern, *The Gender of the Gift*, 3.

8. Ibid., XII and 104.

9. Ibid., 13.

10. To be noted is the fine conceptual development: for Meyer Fortes the person was still a "microcosm of social order," imprint and miniature effect of morality and society. Strathern, on the other hand, uses the term "social microcosm," which constructs no hierarchy between sociality and personality.

11. Strathern, *The Gender of the Gift*, 349.

12. Ibid., 14f, 275f, especially the diagram on page 276. Gender refers to the internal relations between parts of persons, as well as to their externalization as relations between persons. Strathern's focus is on the gendered forms within a person, who appears as either singular or multiple (cf. 185).

13. Ibid., 178f.

14. Cf. ibid., 313.

15. Ibid., 167.

16. Ibid., 132.

17. Ibid.

18. Strathern's anthropological approach, which radically abandons its center, the human being, as center and focuses on the relationships between socialities and things, movements, lines, streams, which are co-emergent with the parts, has also had an important influence on theories going beyond social anthropology, all the way, for instance, to Donna Haraway (*The Companion Species Manifesto. Dogs, People, and Significant Otherness*. Chicago: Prickly Paradigm 2003, 8). For the most recent further developments of Strathern's position, cf. John Frow, *On personhood in public places*, Melbourne: Research Unit in Public Cultures 2012; Casper Bruun Jensen / Kjetil Rodje, "Introduction," in: ibid. (Eds.), *Deleuzian Intersections: Science, Technology, Anthropology*, New York: Berghahn 2012, 1–35; and several of the contributions to the special edition of *Theory, Society & Culture* 31, 2014 on Marilyn Strathern's work. On the other hand, some of what has been written on dividuality in the field of anthropology and ethnology since Strathern and partly in reference to her, remains far behind her theory. Misunderstandings of dividuality as inverse identity instead of a movement of transversing or as a danger for the integrity of the individual, haunt investigations of the dividual almost cyclically. Cf. the conservative, cultural-pessimistic turns of the dividual, for instance in Mark Mosko, "Partible penitents: dividual personhood and Christian practice in Melanesia and the West," in: *Journal of the Royal Anthropological Institute (N.S.)* 16, 2010, 215–240, Karl Smith, "From dividual and individual selves to porous subjects," in: *The Australian Journal of Anthropology* 23, 2012, 50–64, or the essentialist-ecofeminist approach of Maria Mies: without reference to Marilyn Strathern or other feminist sources, Mies develops her discourse on dividuality as the dismembering of the individual and the marketing of the body, its reproducibility and its organs against the backdrop of the "industrial marketing of child production" ("From the Individual to the Dividual: the Supermarket of 'Reproductive Alternatives,'" in: Maria Mies / Vandana Shiva, *Ecofeminism*, London: Zed Books 1993, 198–216).

19. Cormac Cullinan, *Wild Law*, Devon: Green Books 2011, 30. Cf. Also the Earth Democracy Movement in India and the Earth Justice Movement founded in South Africa.

20. Cf. Cullinan, *Wild Law*, 95–98.

21. Ibid., 112 f.

22. Félix Guattari, *Chaosmosis*, translated from French by Paul Bains and Julian Pefanis, Bloomington & Indianapolis: Indiana University Press 1995, 28.

23. Ibid., 118.

24. Boaventura de Sousa Santos, "Law and Community: The Changing Nature of State Power in Late Capitalism," in: *International Journal of the Sociology of Law* 1980, 8, 379–397, here: 390.

25. The term chaosmos is already found in James Joyce's *Finnegans Wake*, and then beginning in the late 1960s in the writings of Gilles Deleuze and Félix Guattari, cf. especially Guattari's last book *Chaosmosis*.

26. Santos, "Law and Community," 391.

27. On the question of constituent power in political history and in the history of political theory, cf. Antonio Negri, *Insurgencies. Constituent Power and the Modern State*, translated from Italian by Maurizia Boscagli, Minneapolis/London: Minnesota 1999.

28. On Venezuela, see Dario Azzelini's works, which further develop Antonio Negri's concept of constituent power, among other ideas, and apply it to the Bolivarian process in Venezuela.

29. Another example of a constituent process is Bolivia, where Evo Morales was the first indigenous person elected to president in 2005. Here too, the procedure of law-making through a new constitution was chosen in 2009. On 22 April 2009, due to Evo Morales' initiative, the same day was declared "International Mother Earth Day" by the UN General Assembly. At a People's World Conference on Climate Change and Mother Earth's Rights a year later in Cochabamba, the Universal Declaration of the Rights of Mother Earth was proclaimed.

30. Magdalena León T., "El 'buen vivir': objetivo y camino para otro modelo," in: Irene León (Ed.), *Sumak Kawsay / Buen Vivir y cambios civilizatorios*, Quito: FEDAEPS 2010, 105–123, here: 107f.

31. In the words of the chairman of the constitutional assembly, Alberto Acosta: "El *Buen Vivir* es entendido como una vida en armonia de los seres humanos consigo mismos, con sus congeneres y con la naturaleza. Asi como tenemos que defender y fortalecer los derechos humanos—y lo venimos haciendo ya 60 anos— es importante pensar en la Declaracion Universal de los Derechos de la Naturaleza. Si no entendemos que la naturaleza es la base de la vida no podemos ni siquiera comenzar a defender los derechos humanos." Alberto Acosta, "Respuestas regionales para problemas globales," in: Irene León (Ed.), *Sumak Kawsay / Buen Vivir y cambios civilizatorios*, Quito: FEDAEPS 2010, 89–104, here 100. Acosta explicitly points out that in the references to indigenous spirituality there is no idea of a mere return to a state before colonialization (cf. ibid., 99). Cf. also the texts on "Políticas del sumak kawsay," in: *Revista de Antropología Experimental* 14, 2014, http://www.ujaen.es/huesped/rae/.

32. Cf. Magdalena León T., "El 'buen vivir,'" 114.

33. Francesco Salvini, "Sumak kawsay or the Politics of Joyful Living, http://eipcp.net/n/1384760094

34. Francesco Salvini (ibid.) uses the free translation "beauty of living together."

35. "Decidimos construir Una nueva forma de convivencia ciudadana, en diversitad y armonía con la naturaleze, para alcanzar el buen vivir, el sumak kawsay."

36. Cf. for instance the contradictions between state-funded extractivism and the juridification of the indigenous demand to live in an ecologically balanced environment in the constitution. A relevant critique of Argentina, Bolivia and Ecuador can be found, among others, in Sandro Mezzadra and Brett Neilson, "Extraction, logistics, finance. Global crisis and the politics of operations," in: *Radical Philosophy* 178, March/April 2013, 8–18.

37. Boaventura de Sousa Santos, "Cuando los excluidos tienen Derecho: justicia indígena, plurinacionalidad e interculturalidad," in: *Justicia indígena, plurinacionalidad e interculturalidad en Ecuador*, Eds. Boaventura de Sousa Santos/ Agustín Grijalva Jiménez, Quito: Abya Yala 2012, 13–50.

38. The two structural dangers do not simply vanish here: instead of an autonomous decision between two laws and two languages in *interlegalidad* and *híbridos jurídicos*, it can happen that one falls into the gap between the two orders and is thus exposed to a situation of disfranchisement/lawlessness. Instead of a breach in the constituted power of traditional law, the chaosmic power of social relationships can be appropriated/overcoded by the state apparatus.

39. In *The Three Ecologies* (translated from French by Chris Turner, *new formations* 8, Summer 1989, 131–147), Félix Guattari mentions these three levels, and in *Chaosmosis* he calls them "three modalities of praxis and subjectivation that correspond to three types of assemblages of enunciation, which in turn comprise equally the psyche, human societies, the living world, the machinic species and, in the final consequence, the cosmos itself." (108)

40. Cf. René Ramirez, "La transición ecuatoriana hacia el Buen Vivir," in: Irene León (Ed.), *Sumak Kawsay / Buen Vivir y cambios civilizatorios*, Quito: FEDAEPS 2010, 125–141, here: 141.

41. A similar figure of the leap between the times, as I would like to read it, is the figure that Guattari calls a "new aesthetic paradigm." He distinguishes between a proto-aesthetic organic paradigm, a capitalist, bipolar-modern paradigm, and a new aesthetic paradigm. The prefixes "proto-" and "new" do not refer here to a linear logic of development and progress. For the new composition of a present aesthetic paradigm, Guattari is also not seeking to pave the way for a return to the holistic ecologies and the "territorialized assemblages of expressions" of the proto-aesthetic paradigm. Cf. Guattari, *Chaosmosis*, 105. The aesthetic paradigm also overlaps with ethical aspects. The good and the beautiful are not to be separated from one another. In this way the aesthetic paradigm becomes an ethico-aesthetic paradigm. Guattari already alluded to the concept of this ethico-aesthetic paradigm in *The Three Ecologies* (132). Here, however, the aspects of the ethical (obligation, influence on instances) and the aesthetic (reinvention) are still analyzed relatively

conventionally and separate from one another, cf. 133. On dividual aesthetics, cf. the works by Michaela Ott, especially her book *Dividuationen*, Berlin: b_books 2015.

42. Deleuze/Guattari, *A Thousand Plateaus*, 6. On the concept of the "molecular revolution," cf. Félix Guattari/Suely Rolnik, *Molecular Revolution in Brazil*, Los Angeles: Semiotext(e) 2007, and Félix Guattari, "Molecular Revolutions and Q&A," in Sylvère Lothinger / David Morris (Eds.), *Schizo-Culture. The Event 1975*, Los Angeles: Semiotext(e) 2013, 184–195.